HOCKEY MADE EASY

BOBBY HULL'S
HOCKEY MADE EASY

WITH ROY G. NELSON

Photography by Paul J. Bereswill

Phil Esposito, Gordie Howe, Bobby Orr, and Bobby Hull race out of their zone
in a Masters of Hockey game as referee Red Storey looks on.

Beaufort Books, Inc.
New York

To those who use hockey as a sport to play, watch, and enjoy—young and old alike!
Bobby Hull

To Rosemarie, Roy, Danny, Michael, and James
Roy Nelson

Design and diagrams by Fortunato Aglialoro
Cover design by Brant Cowie/Artplus Ltd.
Cover photography by Paul J. Bereswill

Published in Canada by Methuen Publications
2330 Midland Avenue, Agincourt, Ontario M1S 1P7
ISBN 0-458-96750-5

First American edition published in the
United States by Beaufort Books Inc., New York
ISBN 0-8253-0226-9

Canadian Cataloguing in Publication Data
Hull, Bobby, 1939–
Bobby Hull's hockey made easy
ISBN 0-458-96750-5

1. Hockey   I. Nelson, Roy.   II. Title
GV847.H84 1983   796.96'2   C83-099202-2

Library of Congress Cataloging in Publication Data
Hull, Bobby.
Bobby Hull's Hockey made easy.
1. Hockey.   I. Nelson, Roy G.   II. Title.   III. Title: Hockey made easy.
GV847.H78 1984   796.9622   84-9242
ISBN 0-8253-0226-9

Printed and bound in Canada by
T. H. Best Printing Company Limited

10 9 8 7 6 5 4 3 2 1

CONTENTS

PREFACE

With its odd lines and circles embedded in the surface of the ice, hockey can be a little forbidding to the first-time player or fan. Bewilderment is understandable and normal. And it's unfortunate that such players and potential fans often don't have parents or friends who are knowledgeable, patient, and willing to take the time to explain all the whistles, stoppages of play, and skills that make up the sport of hockey.

If you are a newcomer to the game, or if you just want to find out the finer points of play, relax. Because here we are going to make hockey easy to understand. The hard work necessary to play it well will be up to you.

The true origin of hockey has been debated for many years; it is a dispute best left to historians. What is more important is that in the century or so in which it has been an organized athletic contest, hockey has become one of the most popular sports in the world.

Today there are many more players involved in organized hockey, from the novice and squirt levels right through to the professional leagues. And as the sport has grown, there have been enormous changes in many areas, one of the most marked being the internationalization of the game.

In Canada, a youngster taking his first steps on the ice soon after learning how to walk has long been part of a way of life. Through this way of life came a near total domination of hockey at the professional levels by Canadians.

But in recent years we have seen the old six-team National Hockey League almost triple through expansion, then gain a rival in the World Hockey Association, which I joined in 1972. The merger of these two leagues created the present twenty-one-team NHL.

This evolution of hockey has brought new opportunities for players and fans alike. Today, we see many more American youngsters playing hockey, and the influx of American and European players into the NHL has become routine. Hockey has most assuredly undergone a dramatic change and become truly an international sport. The 1982–83 National Hockey League had a total of 465 players. Of these, 366 were Canadian, 45 were American, and 54 were born outside North America.

The NHL, a league traditionally resistant to change, has come a long way since its birth in 1917, and undoubtedly will change much more in years to come, perhaps even to the point of adding international teams. Some may doubt that this could happen, but then who would have thought we would see the thrilling contests of a Canada Cup Series?

Violence: A Personal Note

One change in the style of hockey play has not been a welcome one. All too often hockey is associated in the minds of the public with violence, partly because the press exposes incidents of violence more than those of skill. This, unfortunately, serves as a deterrent for many parents when their children want to play the sport. Violence in children's hockey, however, is minimal. It's in the professional leagues that these incidents occur.

In the professional ranks, a man's job is at stake, and anger and frustration sometimes result in violence. But there is no doubt that young children are influenced by professional players and in some instances closely emulate their style of play. Therefore, it is an important obligation of professional players to set an example for the young to follow.

And it is extremely important for the individuals who organize and control leagues to make every possible effort to eliminate or at least restrict the amount of free-wheeling, bully play that is sometimes evident in the NHL and is even a tactic used deliberately by some teams. In a sport that has constant body contact at high speeds, an attempt to completely eliminate fighting probably would be futile, but bully behaviour must be limited.

Efforts *have* been made to address the problem of violence in hockey. In 1982 a conference, "War and Violence in North America (Sacks, Strikes, and Slapshots)," was held in Toronto. (Interestingly enough, hockey was not the only sport addressed.) This conference concluded that through the efforts of league officials and concerned players, violent outbursts could be practically eliminated. Perhaps it would help to make all rinks conform to the international standard. The wider rink would eliminate the poor skaters, those with nothing but intimidation on their minds, planted there by incompetent team officials.

Strong efforts by coaches and management to restrict these actions by players is in the best interest of the sport, its participants, and the fans. Hockey is a rough sport, and not for the faint-hearted, but it should not be viewed as a gladiatoral contest.

It is understandable that parents would be concerned about possible injury to their children. This is a concern in every sport that children play, and is not limited to hockey. But parents should not allow this concern to develop into intense worry that would be detrimental not only to the parent but also to the youngster playing the sport. It is impossible for a player to achieve his full potential when playing with a constant fear of injury. Such fear interferes with the absolute concentration and free body movement that are necessary to play the game well.

Bobby Hull, 1983

9

INTRODUCTION

From frozen lakes and ponds in small towns to arenas in large metropolitan cities, no sport has so captured the imagination and interest of people as has hockey. Young and old pass through the turnstiles of arenas throughout the world to witness one of sport's greatest spectacles, a game whose fast pace, continuous action, excitement, and colour are unmatched by any other. What once began as a uniquely Canadian sport is now played all over the United States and has also gained international popularity.

When the exuberant and excited fans pass through the turnstiles they will see, silent before them, a rectangular, glazed surface of ice, bordered by glass. When the game begins, this surface will form the field of battle for a fierce and determined athlete—the hockey player.

Within the confines of these borders, players travel at speeds of over 20 miles per hour and propel a six-ounce disk of vulcanized rubber at speeds of over 100 miles per hour! Who can doubt that hockey is the fastest sport in the world?

Through mass media coverage, sellout crowds, and the enormous growth of hockey schools and teams at all age levels, it is obvious that ice hockey is the sport of the '80s. The need for a definitive instructional text to match this interest and growth has become apparent.

To young spectators who come with wide eyes and big dreams, hockey provides heroes in whose footsteps they hope to follow someday.

Along with this enthusiasm comes a thirst for knowledge about hockey that, for a young mind, is hard to quench. There is no reason why the young fan searching for knowledge should be frustrated by the unavailability of complete and readily accessible information.

This book, with its thorough analysis of the game, provided by one of hockey's greatest all-time stars, will offer the information that all fans, young and old, want about the sport they love. Its Flip-a-Skill format, which offers explicit illustrations of proper playing techniques, will also allow young players to teach themselves in a way that has never been possible before.

This book can be used by coaches of young players, by fans who wish to increase their appreciation of the game, by parents who may be unfamiliar with the sport and who wish to learn more about their children's interests, and by players who wish to refine their skills and improve their performance.

Parents especially should take note that hockey not only helps players develop team spirit and play, individual achievement, determination, perseverance, the commitment necessary to achieve success, and the maturity to accept victory or defeat graciously, but also improves their peripheral vision, balance, and coordination. Hockey's role in youngsters' development of motor skills and muscular development is unparalleled.

So, whether you intend to play the game or merely to learn more about it, this book will be your passport to the exciting world of hockey.

Roy Nelson, 1983

9

1
THE
BASICS

Learning how to play a sport is a challenge that should be met with an open mind and a positive attitude. Sometimes, though, budding players begin the task with the attitude that they already "know it all" or that the game will be "a cinch" to learn. With this kind of poor attitude, the reality of playing can come as a shock. This is unfortunate and unnecessary. If you pay attention to the basics of hockey as outlined in this book and prepare yourself before going out on the ice, the game will become not only easier to learn, but also a lot more fun to watch and to play.

Before we embark on learning how to play the game, let's take a closer look at some other aspects of hockey.

The hockey rink looks like this:

Hockey is played in three twenty-minute periods. The object of the game is to manoeuvre the puck into the opposing team's net or goal, for which the scoring team receives one point.

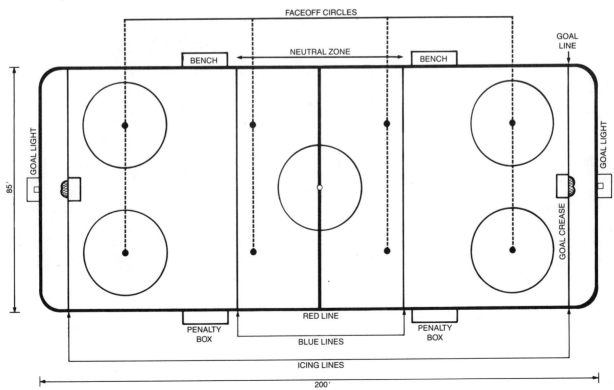

The hockey net is constructed like this:

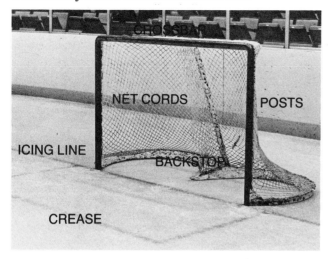

The hockey team consists of six players (with twelve alternates on the bench, including an extra goaltender) in the following positions:

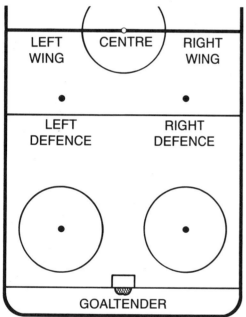

Rules

To explain all the rules that govern hockey would require a whole book, but a look at three basic rules is worthwhile. These rules directly govern the flow of play and will be helpful to you when we discuss offensive and defensive play.

Icing the Puck The puck cannot be "iced," or shot from one side of the red line across the opposing team's goal line, when the teams are at full strength. If a team does so, the result is an icing call when a member of the opposing team touches the puck after it has passed over the goal line. The puck is brought back to the offending team's end for a faceoff where play begins again.

There are certain exceptions to the icing rule. Icing is not called:
- When the goaltender touches the puck after it crosses the goal line.
- When the icing team has a penalty.
- When an opposing player can touch the puck before it crosses the goal line but does not do so. In this case, icing is called off or waved off by the linesmen and play continues.
- When the puck crosses through the goaltender's crease.
- When a player from the icing team beats the opposition player to the puck and touches it first after the puck passes over the goal line.

Offside An offside occurs when a member of one team precedes the puck across the blue line of the opposing team. The puck must enter the zone first, then the attacking players can freely follow it.

A player on the attacking team can straddle the blue line, that is, have one skate on one side of the blue line and one on the other side and not be called offside, since both skates must be in the defending team's zone for an offside to occur. This type of rule controls entry into the attacking zone and restricts the attacking forwards from getting behind the defencemen before the puck enters their zone.

The blue-line straddle as a perfect onside pass approaches.

The Offside Pass A player cannot pass from behind his own blue line to a teammate standing over the red line. This rule controls attacking forwards from "hanging" at the red line for long passes and a quick break in on net.

Play is also stopped for the following infractions or penalties, which remove the offending player from the ice for a specified period of time, most often two minutes. The penalized player returns to the ice either when his penalty time is up or when a goal is scored by the opposing team. For a complete look at the rules of hockey, consult the official National Hockey League Rules.

Elbowing   Slowwhistle   Charging   Slashing

Misconduct   Delayed Calling of Penalty   Crosschecking   Holding

Icing   Boarding   Washout   Interference

Hooking   Tripping

Equipment

To play properly, you must have the proper equipment. The equipment used in hockey today is light and conforms to the body with a great degree of flexibility, increasing protection and allowing you a great deal of agility.

The completely equipped hockey player on an organized team should have an athletic protector, garter belt, shin pads, hockey stockings, padded hockey shorts (to protect the thighs, hips, and tailbone), shoulder pads, elbow pads, and protective hockey gloves.

What we'll cover here are the three basic items that are the most important pieces of equipment whether you're playing on a team at an arena or just playing shinny in the back yard.

Skates   The first item to buy, of course, is a pair of hockey skates. All too often, because of cost, parents provide children with hand-me-down skates, use skates provided in rinks for skating sessions, or buy skates several sizes too large in order to last a growing child for several seasons. These will serve for occasional skating, but the young player should not skate regularly with someone else's skates or on skates not fitted properly.

Rink skates are often worn out and will not provide proper support. This can put unnecessary strain on the feet and legs, as well as cause injuries. Skates handed down by older family members have likely been broken in to the skating form of the first wearer, and can therefore hamper the development of the first-time skater. (Double runners are sometimes used to introduce the very young to skating. I don't encourage their use, because they give a youngster a false sense of security.)

It is best for the first-time skater to be fitted properly with skates as near to his size as possible, and which will afford the necessary protection and comfort. A careful inspection prior to buying any skates will ensure good value, protection, and support. If you have suffered the experience of hand-me-downs and rink skates, you will be amazed during your first time on properly fitted skates! Your ankles will stay erect when supported properly, and you can concentrate on refining your skating ability.

Sharpening. Skate blades should always be kept sharp so that there is an edge on the blade. This provides the necessary grip on the ice so that you can push off easily. If the blades are dull, they will not grip the ice properly and unnecessary spills will result.

Have respect for your skates. Try not to have your blades come in contact with anything but the ice you skate on, or the soft material you walk on in dressing rooms or on your way to the ice. Constant sharpening is not necessary, but when you find an edge has been burred, causing you to slip or fall when you turn or stop, be sure to have your skates sharpened.

A good rink skate sharpener, besides being worth his weight in gold to players, will also follow your sharpening instructions and provide you with the desired radius or rocker—the degree of curve on the blade—for each player. Too short a rocker causes instability and a teetering effect. You should have at least 2½ to 3½ inches of blade on the ice.

Parts of the Skate. The toes of the skates are usually made of a hard substance to protect the player's toes from other players' skate blades and sticks, and from the puck.

A rear view of the tendon guards.

The tendon guard protects the back of the heel—the Achilles tendon—which could be severed by an opposing player's skate.

The lacing of the skate should be wide so that the fit is comfortable and evenly proportioned throughout the skate.

Wide lacing (left) and an improper narrow lacing (right).

You might hear stories of professional players placing their skates into a bucket of warm water to get a proper fit. This does occur, since some players believe this is the way to get the boot to fit snugly to the foot. But this is an extreme measure and should not be followed by the beginner.

Skates represent your initial investment in hockey, so it is important that this investment be made wisely through an established sporting-goods store, which will also provide excellent advice from trained sports sales people who can fit the foot of the new skater properly.

Again, it is important that the skates be comfortable. The length of time on the ice should not be hampered by ill-fitting skates which could also cause injury. No skater should have to suffer blisters or sores because of an improper fit, then have to skate the next day in extreme discomfort. All this can easily be avoided by a little time and effort.

The Stick After choosing the proper skates, you are ready to choose the proper hockey stick. Sticks are available in right-handed, left-handed, and neutral styles.

The proper length of the stick can be determined by standing in your skates with the tip of the blade of the stick on the floor. The butt end of the stick should reach your chin. (If you are in stocking feet, the butt end should be up to your nose.) This is just a handy "rule of thumb" and, depending on your individual skating style, the length can be adjusted. If you skate close to the ice you will need a shorter stick; if you skate more upright you will need a longer one.

A hockey stick consists of the following parts: the heel; the curve, mid-point, or cup; the butt end; the toe; and the shaft. Hockey sticks traditionally had blades with only a slight bend to differentiate between the left- and right-handed shooter, with straight blades neutral. The invention of the curved or banana blade led to many variations in curvature, though in the NHL and many minor league associations the curve of the blade cannot exceed one-half inch.

Notice the curve of the blade and the tape from tip to heel.

A heavily curved blade can give greater velocity to a shot when handled by talented players, by allowing them to receive the puck and release it in a flinging motion. But only a slight curve or none at all should be used by the novice player still in the process of learning the game.

Taping the Stick. Tape is placed on the butt and blade of the hockey stick to serve four basic functions: (1) to provide a knob at the butt end of the stick so that you do not lose your grip on the stick, especially when you are carrying the puck with one hand or attempting to take the puck from an opposing player; (2) to provide protection and a cushion for the puck when a hard pass is received; (3) to provide a target for a teammate passing the puck to aim at; and (4) to provide you with a method of hiding the puck from the view of the

15

goaltender. Because the tape and the puck are both black, a goaltender may not be able to distinguish clearly between them until you shoot the puck—and by then it may be too late!

The taping of hockey sticks varies as much as players do, for hockey players are very individual-

Here the end, or butt, of the shaft is taped.

istic in their attempts to gain scoring advantages. Each player must find out what works best for him. My own suggestion would be to tape the entire blade with black friction tape from within an inch of the toe to the heel. (For reason 4 above, it makes no sense to tape the stick with white tape.)

Flexibility. The stick must have a degree of flexibility called "whip." This flexibility is tested by holding the hockey stick in both hands (as in the shooting position), placing the blade on the ground or ice, and bending the stick by leaning your weight on it. A flexible stick will return to its original position with a quick snapping motion or whip when you release the pressure of your weight. In shooting, the whip or snap will give you greater velocity when the shot is completed, since the whip is then moving in the direction of the target with the full force of your weight and the snap of your wrists, forearms, and upper body behind the shot.

Holding the Hockey Stick   With the proper grip, the stick becomes an extension of your body through your hands and arms, communicating your thoughts to the puck. The hockey stick also gives you better balance. After playing for hours with a stick in your hands, you will find it strange to skate without one.

The proper way to tape the stick blade.

The grip of the stick in the traditional hockey stance.

When shooting right-handed, the left hand is placed at the butt of the stick shaft with the fist facing forward and the right hand midway down the shaft in a comfortable position with the palm facing forward. For a left-handed shooter, the right hand is high and the left part way down the shaft.

Clasp the fingers and thumb firmly around the stick, but keep them loose enough to slide up and down the shaft of the stick during different sequences of shooting. This position should be a comfortable one, and if you find it difficult to make proper contact with the puck and ice you should consider changing the *lie* of the stick (the angle at which the blade meets the ice compared to the handle) or the length of the stick.

Helmets Helmets have become common in professional hockey and are now mandatory in children's hockey.

The degree of protection offered by these helmets far outweighs the discomfort that some players say they cause. It is true that some players, myself included, who didn't wear helmets in their early days could find that a helmet causes a great deal of obstruction or restriction. This is a valid complaint and could hinder a player's performance dramatically. But the introduction of these helmets to very young players will contribute to their acceptance in the professional ranks, as we can already see today.

The "bird cages" that attach to these helmets help to reduce eye injuries from sticks and pucks.

Also available are mouthpieces which, after being softened with warm water, will conform to the child's tooth formation when placed in his mouth. This mouthpiece should be worn for every play.

These protective devices have done much to reduce hockey injuries, and parents should make sure their child uses them. Helmets, elbow pads, and gloves are the three most important pieces of protective equipment a player can use. Try not to venture on the ice without them.

Practice

Many of the techniques and skills you'll read about in this book might seem complicated at first, and they may be difficult to accomplish too. But recall the times you never thought you'd be able to do something—like ride a bike, or pass a test in school. It seemed insurmountable. But what a joy when you conquered it! The same is true of hockey, but remember, you only get out of something what you put into it. If you work hard, it will pay off in the long run.

The more time you spend on the ice, the faster you will learn to play the game well. So practise the techniques. Don't become discouraged. Be patient and keep trying.

A useful word to remember when playing is SAFETY, which stands for Setup, Approach, Follow-through, Execution, Timing, and You. These are the words to bear in mind for effective performance. And they will make learning a new skill much easier.

Shinny Games played on outdoor patches of ice, from neighbourhood rinks to frozen ponds, are called "shinny" and tend to be more loosely organized than those played in arenas. Groups of people play without definite teams and each player tries to get the puck (which may be just a piece of ice, a rock, or some other hard object) from whoever is controlling it. Play goes back and forth for hours.

Someone viewing this disorganized madness might ask, "What useful purpose does it serve for people to run about the ice without a proper goal and without teams?"

But shinny, especially for young players, provides a significant foundation for future hockey growth. During these games the young player learns to dodge many opponents and to keep control of the puck. He also learns the art of stickhandling and other ways of controlling the puck while he is skating. Because of the great numbers of players, each trying to get the puck from the player who has it and willing to knock down anyone in the way, the shinny player also learns the valuable skill of playing with his head up. Finally, shinny encourages youngsters to try new things, which a more structured environment sometimes allows only under pressure or not at all.

The benefits gained from playing shinny can be seen when you play an organized game and are subjected to fewer opponents, a confined area in which to play, and rules, which on an outdoor rink or pond are often ignored.

Youngsters who do not have the obvious advantage of playing with this freedom suffer, because being good at hockey requires personal creativity.

Team Practices Skill comes with time. No one is expected to emerge from a sporting-goods store with a complete hockey outfit and be automatically a master of all aspects of hockey. However, the player who concerns himself with refining his weak areas will progress much more quickly than the player who only concentrates on his strengths. The best circumstance for training, of course, is in practice, where mistakes can be made with the least amount of liability to one's team and personal performance. It is here that coaches should stress constructive criticism, which you should take as a learning opportunity, not a putdown. You should be willing to admit that you don't understand the coach or that you can't accomplish the move requested of you. By being honest with the coach and admitting your weaknesses, you can benefit from the coach's criticism and advice on how to improve your ability by exercise, further refinement of your skating skills, or just plain hard work.

Both the team and the individual player will benefit from the coach's instruction and the time spent during training sessions.

All too often, teams do not or are not able to conduct regular training sessions as the pros do, or to practise before games. This is a problem for the player who must refine most of his skills during an actual game and does not have the advantage of trying things out in practice. If your team is not getting enough practice time, you should take your skates and stick to the nearest rink or pond and work on your skating and puck-handling skills, either by yourself or with a few friends. Every bit of extra ice time will help you improve your game.

Off Ice   You can practise techniques off the ice as well as on. Street hockey and roller hockey have become very popular sports. Both can refine and develop a young player's skills for ice hockey. Kent Nilsson of the Calgary Flames spends several hours a day during the summer months practising his shooting off a concrete pad into a net curtain—and we all know how Kent can rip the puck.

These offshoots of ice hockey also have certain drawbacks. In street and roller hockey, the puck is much lighter than in ice hockey. This can give you some problems in adjusting your timing on the ice. Therefore, you must develop your wrists and forearms to obtain the necessary strength in your arms for ice hockey. But on the whole, street hockey and roller hockey will help your ice hockey game far more than they will hurt it—just be aware of the differences between playing on and off the ice, and compensate for them.

Some interesting variations of conditioning and off-ice practice have developed in recent years. Brought about by lack of on-ice practice, some have proved to be not only worthy substitutes, but

also primary training techniques.

Soccer, for example, has become a way to teach positional play and the all-important skill of accepting passes with your feet while skating. All European and Soviet players are very adept at this. Soccer also conditions players while still maintaining a sports and team environment that resembles hockey.

One way to sharpen a goaltender's reflexes is to shoot tennis balls instead of pucks at him. His ability to react to the ball's curves and skips off the ground can be an effective substitute for on-ice practice.

Conditioning   To say that training has changed in recent years would be an understatement. But one thing remains true: you must be physically fit to play a sport well and to be protected against injuries. (Even for people who don't play a sport, it's nice to feel healthy and strong!) Use of the Bobby Hull Life Line Gym can help condition the body without the stiffness and bulk that sometimes result from traditional weightlifting; a few simple exercises following the instructions included with the Life Line Gym will help you do it.

**Includes Chapter on
Rehabilitation of Sports Injuries**

2 SKATING

Skating is the most important skill in hockey, because the ability to control your movements on the ice provides the foundation to which all other skills are added. Natural ability plays a large part in learning to skate, and you should be aware of your own body movements so that you may evaluate and develop your individual style. Skating is hard work, but fun when you have taken the time to learn it properly. Don't hide in the back of the pack and coast along during skating drills, for your lack of effort will surely become evident in your play. For remember, simply put, skating is hockey and hockey is skating!

Many first-time skaters fear that their ankles will be too weak to maintain balance, and, of course, they also worry about falling on the ice. It is unlikely that you will have any problems with weak ankles as long as your skates are properly fitted so that they give your ankles the support they need. And while you are bound to have your ups and downs on the ice at first, as you put in more and more hours of skating practice your balance will improve and you will be less and less likely to fall.

As well as developing your skating muscles and skills in practice, you will also be developing your heart and lungs, which is so very important for an athlete's stamina and endurance.

Powerful skating is made up of: (1) proper conditioning, (2) balance, (3) fluid movement, (4) long strides, (5) hard work, and (6) a certain amount of natural ability. It is extremely important that a player's natural ability be developed to its fullest potential. Achieving this goal will pay many important dividends later on.

An accomplished skater, such as Marc Messier of Edmonton or Denis Savard of Chicago, gliding effortlessly across the ice, is a beautiful sight to watch. Let's see how this happens.

Skating Forward

Position and Balance Start by standing in the forward skating position. In this position, your knees are slightly bent and the upper body is placed slightly forward with the skates approximately shoulder width apart and hips square. If you forget this forward lean and lean backwards, you will lose your balance, so remember to keep this posture. Once you feel comfortable in this position, flex your knees and body in order to feel movement on the skates.

When you are skating, your legs will alternate between two positions: (1) the forward or striding leg and (2) the back or trailing leg, which pushes off or drives to provide accelerating power.

The Stride Push off with one leg (which then becomes the trailing leg) from the standing position. Do this by bending the knee of the trailing leg and placing its skate blade at an angle on the ice. With your weight on the inside of the blade, straighten the bent knee of the trailing leg. As the blade digs into the ice, extend your ankle and push off from the toe of the blade.

At the same time that all this happens, your striding leg will begin to glide. As you lean forward, your weight will shift to the striding leg from the trailing leg. This shift of body weight will lessen the resistance to the push-off and give you additional momentum.

Now bring your trailing leg to the front of your body by turning your hip on the trailing-leg side to the direction of your first stride. At the same time bring your skate around to the front in a smooth motion. The toe of the blade should hit the ice first, followed by the heel of the blade. This leg should now be in front of your bent upper body, and your knee should be bent. This completes the forward stride.

At this point, the trailing leg has become the striding leg and the striding leg is now the trailing leg. You are now ready to push off or drive in the same fashion as your first push-off.

Drive off with the right leg, as your body weight shifts to the striding leg.

Speed. Speed is initially achieved by the power of the drives of the trailing leg, and can be increased by coordinating other body motions with these movements.

When you become confident of your ability to maintain balance while alternating strides in the forward skating position, you can skate faster by increasing the number of strides. Shifting your weight in a rhythm with these movements will give you a further increase in speed, as well as a fluid motion that is repeated and coordinated with hip and upper body movement. For example, when a greater amount of weight is placed on the trailing leg at the time of the push-off, the strength of the push is maximized, since the weight against this leg pushes the body in the opposite direction. If the weight were placed on the front leg at the time of push-off, resistance to the forward movement of the body would be increased, and the

power of the push-off would be dramatically reduced. So the release of the weight from one leg to the other must be timed perfectly in order to be effective.

If you can successfully coordinate your alternating shift of weight from one leg to the other with your alternating swing of the hips (which represent your centre of gravity) you will achieve proper balance and also be able to use the full strength of your legs.

Your weight is shifted to the right leg.

Now your weight is shifted to the left leg.

Your upper body also plays an important role in skating. The alternating swings of your arms and shoulders correspond to the movements of your legs and, when they are properly coordinated, give greater momentum and strength to your stride.

Keep your skates as close as possible to the ice when you execute these movements so that you lose the least amount of time between strides. Keep your body lower to the ice, too. This generates a stronger centre of push for the trailing leg and provides a better position from which to execute more complicated skating techniques. When you perform these movements properly you will feel the power from the drive in your trailing leg and the smoothness of the glide in your striding leg while maintaining proper balance.

Breathing. Take rhythmic and natural breaths so that fresh air circulates throughout your lungs. Your breathing need not be pronounced, but should be deep enough to provide a sufficient amount of oxygen.

Do not bend forward too much or else you will cut off your air supply. If you do not get enough oxygen you will tire quickly.

When full coordination of these body movements has been mastered, you can then determine your particular skating style and identify your strong or weak points. One common weakness is favouring one side over another, which can come through skating only in one direction during practice sessions. Favouring one side is natural, and hard work is required to correct it. But you must make the effort to improve your ability on the weak side; the results will make it seem worthwhile.

The Forward Crossover The forward crossover is sometimes neglected by skaters because it is a difficult manoeuvre to master without practice. But agility with speed is essential in hockey, and the benefits of the forward crossover are immeasurable, for it is a quick method of changing direction while skating in the forward position.

It is accomplished by placing the striding leg diagonally across and over the trailing leg in front of your body, at the same time turning and dropping the shoulder on the side of the striding leg over in the same direction. As this occurs the trailing leg sweeps across in back of the striding leg to give you additional power. This causes you to turn quickly and skate in the direction of the crossover. A similar crossover with the now trailing leg in the opposite direction of the first crossover will bring you back to your original skating path. A second crossover in the same direction will take you further into the turn.

The forward crossover may seem hard to visualize, especially since you were just introduced to the challenge of the forward skate. But, as you remember, in the forward skate you kept your weight on one side at a time. This was done for a reason, since you thus became used to bearing weight on one foot at a time while maintaining balance. This has prepared you to bring one foot over and across as in the crossover.

As your striding foot hits the ice, your weight should automatically shift to this foot until you assume the forward skating position or stop.

The start of the forward crossover. Your weight is placed on the striding right leg as the trailing left leg is lifted off the ice.

The left leg is now brought over and across the right (now the trailing) leg.

Now the left leg has fully crossed over the right leg and has become the striding leg.

This movement is used: (1) to avoid an oncoming opponent and regain your original direction quickly, (2) to turn, or (3) to gain speed quickly.

Remember, to be effective this skill must be executed with smooth rhythmic movements and the trailing leg must drive in a smooth *sideways* movement, instead of front to back.

If performed properly, this manoeuvre will bring your body close to the ice, and the zigs and zags of its movement will resemble someone quickly weaving in and out. This pattern is not accidental—its purpose is to help you avoid defenders, and this weaving motion can be an extremely deceptive one. The weave reduces the target you represent, and at any time you can come out of this movement by a further crossover to your original direction or away from the direction of the defender.

The forward crossover requires strong legs, proper conditioning, and balance, so your initial skating drills provide a necessary foundation for this skill.

Turning The turn is used to change direction with the least loss of momentum. As in the crossover, place the weight of your body on the outer skate edge of the inside leg in the direction in which you intend to turn. For example, in turning right, (1) place your weight in the direction of the turn and on your right leg and, (2) while maintaining the bent-leg position, cross over with the outside (left) leg and push off with the right leg as it becomes the trailing leg. Repeat these crossovers in the same direction to complete the turn.

It is important to note that the turn and the crossover differ in the distribution of your weight. By placing your entire weight on the inside leg, you accomplish a complete turn, whereas in the crossover, the weight shift is momentary to

create only a *temporary* change in position and direction.

The turn can be quickly adjusted by alternating skates in a double crossover. This would bring you back to your original path.

Two-foot turn. The two-foot turn is a wide, sweeping turn, accomplished by placing your skates together with both legs slightly bent and leaning your body in the direction you wish to turn. To come out of the turn, straighten your body away from the lean.

The start of the two-foot turn to the left: feet together, body leaning in the direction of the turn.

In the turn.

The two-foot turn coming around the net.

Coming out of the turn. Your body starts to straighten as the inside leg pushes off.

A two-foot turn to the right.

Fast Starts A sudden burst of energy is needed to generate speed, especially from a standing position. A simple method of attaining quick speed from this position, bringing you to top stride quickly with the least expenditure of energy, is to take several small, quick strides before proceeding with your natural stride. Take short steps from the bent-leg position and dig your blades into the ice. This movement allows you maximum acceleration in a minimum amount of space and conserves energy.

Coasting Since using energy needlessly is a concern of players, your ability to coast or keep moving for periods of time without having to stop or stride and strain muscles is a considerable asset. A proper distribution of weight will allow you to maintain momentum by coasting or gliding.

Coasting with no striding or bend in body movement conserves energy. Keep head up looking at the play.

Pivoting Pivoting allows you to turn quickly in either direction by placing your weight on one skate (on the side you wish to pivot to) while quickly turning your hips and shoulders in a semicircle. The other skate stops the pivot or, when turned with the pivoting skate, moves the entire body in the direction of the pivot.

Scooting To get a quick start, use only the back skate to push off with several sudden thrusts, leaving your front skate in the forward position and your body facing sideways. Keep both knees bent. This method lets you face the play while moving forward. If the direction of the play should change, you can stop your forward movement by turning the front skate sideways and stopping the push-offs.

Stopping

Stopping is probably one of the most difficult skills to attempt at first. To stop, you must place your skates in a different direction (sideways) from your forward movement. To do so without toppling over at first seems impossible. Have no fear, but beware: you must continue your bent-knee posture to maintain balance, proper execution, and control over the stop.

The Two-Foot Stop   To stop with two feet, place your skates together (with both knees bent) and gradually turn them, your hips, and your shoulders sideways in the direction of the stop. Be sure to place your weight evenly on each skate blade and lean away from the direction of the stop. At the same time straighten your knees. This digs the blades of your skates into the ice and causes you to stop. The amount of pressure of the blade on the ice created by the straightening of the knees controls the swiftness of the stop.

Since you can stop by turning sideways to the left or right, your preference and strength will dictate which side is used. You *must* practise stopping on both sides to eliminate favouring one side in a game.

The two-foot stop. The body leans away from the stop as the knees are straightened.

Side view of the two-foot stop.

Once you have come to a full stop you can return to the forward skating position by simply turning your hips back to the square forward position while keeping your skates stationary. The shift in your body's position will return your skates to the forward position.

One-Foot Stop and Turnaround   Stopping by using only one foot gives you the ability to move quickly in the opposite direction of the stop without having to come to a full stop. Although a somewhat difficult manoeuvre, it has many advantages.

Place your weight on the inside left leg to start the stop.

Lean away from the stop and straighten your knee.

Turn your hips, shoulders, and one skate sideways in the direction of the forward movement. Place all your weight on this inside skate (the skate now furthest from your forward movement) and lean away from the stop with your other skate slightly off the ice. As your knee is straightened and your forward progress is slowed, cross the skate off the ice over the inside skate and at the same time turn your hip in the same direction. This allows you to return to the forward skating position without coming to a full stop with two feet.

Bring your right leg over and across the left, turning your shoulder and hip to complete the turnaround.

As you gain forward momentum from the crossover of the front skate, your inside leg is quickly straightened and your weight now shifts to the forward skate. You are now ready to take a stride forward with the stopping (inside) skate.

Toeing-in Stop or Slowdown By placing your weight on the insides of your blades with the toes of your skates at a V angle, keeping your knees slightly bent, and keeping your body in the forward skating position, you can reduce your speed gradually and stop completely without changing the forward position of your body. This allows you to glide with the flow of play or be in a better position to shoot or receive a pass. Again, the quickness of the stop or slowdown is controlled by the amount of pressure you exert on the blades of your skates by straightening your bent knees.
Slowing down with one foot. If you extend your trailing leg behind you so that the entire skate blade drags along the ice, you can control the speed of your forward movement without moving your body or both skates. In this way you can reposition your skates if you wish to change direction or stop.

Jumpstops Jumpstops are accomplished by jumping with both skates in the air and at the same time turning your entire body sideways in the direction of the stop. When your skates hit the ice your entire weight hits too. This is a difficult

manoeuvre and takes time to master, so don't try it right away; have patience and learn the simpler stops first.

Skating Backwards

Skating backwards is a difficult skill to master, since you cannot see where you are going, and the technique is completely different from skating forward. While moving backwards you must also be able to gain speed quickly and be agile enough to keep up with the approach of players who are skating forward at top speed.

Again, a bent-knee position is employed, but with a much more exaggerated crouch. Push your buttocks out while bending your knees as in a sitting position, and lean forward with the remaining portion of your upper body. Swing your hips in an exaggerated movement back and forth. Distribute your weight to the inside of each skate blade and accelerate with each swing of the hips.

Hold your stick in one hand in front of your body. Keep your other hand at your side. Keep your skates on the ice as much as possible, and also keep them further apart than in the forward skating position. This will help you maintain balance and strength for checking. Move your skate blades in unison when you skate straight back and keep your weight on the inner blade distributed from the toe of the blade to the heel as you swing your hips. You can gain speed by moving your hips and skates rapidly, and you will get more drive by slightly straightening your knees as your hips are swayed back and forth.

The backward skating position: (1) knees bent, (2) weight over the knees forward, (3) buttocks out, (4) hands at sides, (5) stick out front.

Backward skating: hips swung to the left.

Skates moved in unison.

Hips swung to the right.

Stopping While Skating Backwards As in forward skating, you must be able to stop your movement while skating backwards.

Two-foot stop. In the two-foot stop, skating forward, your body leaned back and away from the stop. The reverse occurs in the backward stop, i.e., you move forward and away from the stop. As you prepare to stop, place your skates in a V position a comfortable width apart with your toes facing out. Keep your knees bent, your skate blades at an angle to the ice with your weight on the insides of the blades, and your body leaning forward. As you straighten your knees, your blades will dig into the ice and your backward movement will stop.

Two-foot stop (backwards): knees bent with weight forward.

One-foot stop or slowdown. In some situations a player skating backwards needs to change direction quickly to the forward position without coming to a complete stop.

To accomplish this, turn your body slightly to the side while skating backwards. At the same time, place the inside skate sideways with your knee bent. As the knee is straightened the backward movement slows; now bring the back skate forward by placing it over the stopping leg, just before you completely stop. Shift your weight to the leg crossing over and start moving forward without coming to a complete stop. A crossover with the stopping leg will put your body in the full forward skating position.

Backward Crossover A defenceman skating backwards needs not only speed but also sideways movement. This is achieved by the backward crossover.

When skating backwards, place the leg on the side to which you wish to move behind yourself by putting your weight on the inside of your skate blade. This provides the push and power to drive your body to the side. Keep the other skate stationary, with the toe pointed in the direction opposite the movement so that the rear portion of the blade is facing in the direction of the sideways movement and can accept the drive from the leg being crossed over backwards. The movement of this leg is done with a gliding sweeping sideways motion. Continue the crossover until you reach the position you want. Position both skates to meet the attacker.

Naturally, the speed of these crossovers dictates the quickness of the sideways movement, and their number, the change in position.

To return to the full backward skating position, you must do a single backward crossover with the stationary leg. This will make both skates parallel and face your body forward so that you can continue skating backwards in a straight line.

Backward crossover: the right leg sweeps behind and across the left leg.

Turning While Skating Backwards There are three basic categories of backward turns: (1) turning to the forward skating position while skating backwards, (2) turning to the backward skating position while skating forward, and (3) the sweeping turn backwards.

Since you must be able to adjust your skating direction quickly to the flow of play, these three turns must be executed with precision.

Turning to the forward position. To turn to the forward skating position while skating backwards, you must pivot on one foot (the foot in the direction you wish to turn). Allow this leg to trail slightly behind your body, and place your weight on the toe of the pivoting skate. As you straighten your body from the crouched position, turn your hips and shoulders in the direction of the pivot and cross the other skate over the pivoting skate.

Use this manoeuvre when an attacking skater has got past you and you must try to catch him, or any time you wish to skate in the forward position.

While skating backwards, start the pivot by placing your weight on the left leg in the direction of the turn.

Pivot the left shoulder and hip as you release the weight of the pivoting foot.

Return the weight to the pivoting foot (now forward) as you complete the turn.

Turning to the backward skating position. To turn backwards from a forward position, you must pivot your entire body 180°. This pivot is accomplished by placing your weight on the tip of your pivoting blade (which is slightly ahead of your body) at the point of the pivot. Turn your hips and shoulders around to the backward skating position using the weight of the pivot to turn and support your body. Your weight is then evenly distributed on both skate blades.

As you bend your knees to cushion your weight, extend your buttocks to assume the backward skating position. The momentum of your body weight carries your body backwards with your arms at your sides, stick extended to the front in the full backward skating position. It is important that your pivot be smooth and graceful, otherwise you will lose your balance and perhaps fall. Even a second used to regain balance may be enough to let the attacker go around you.

Skating forward: the pivot starts with the weight on the right leg.

The body continues to turn right 180°.

Halfway into the turn, the left leg returns to the ice.

The body completes its swing, with both skates on the ice.

Sweeping turn backwards. In some situations it is advantageous to turn gradually while still facing the oncoming attackers. You may want to (1) see your teammates, (2) stop retreating into your zone without having to turn around or come to a complete stop, and (3) increase your range of sideways movement with the sweep.

This movement is accomplished in the same manner as the sideways crossover—except that at the point where you would normally do a reverse crossover to bring you back to a backward skating position, you have three alternatives. First, you can stop by placing the blade of the skate on the side of your sweeping turn, bending your knees and digging the blade into the ice while straightening up (this will allow you to skate forward or backwards). Second, you can skate forward by stopping your backward crossover and with the next stride stepping into a forward skating motion. At the time you take the forward stride, quickly move the shoulder and hip on the same side to the forward position. Cross the stationary leg backwards to restrict the movement and, at the end of the crossover, push or drive off toward the forward direction by straightening your bent knee. The third alternative is to continue with the sweeping turn.

This manoeuvre obviously minimizes your loss of momentum and keeps you in a position to see the play and, if you have possession of the puck, to pass it at any point or skate with it yourself.

Adding the Stick   Since you have practised these skating exercises without a stick, using one will increase your balance and lead us to our next subject—puck control. Remember that the stick should be kept low to the ice in most instances. It can be held with either one or two hands, depending on the playing situation.

The reasons for keeping your stick low to the ice are (1) to give a target for a pass, (2) to be ready for a shot, and (3) to skate safely without causing injury to other players on the ice.

Power Skating

Throughout this chapter I have stressed the importance of balance because balance gives you stability. Stability is extremely important since it allows you to take body checks without being completely removed from the play, and allows you to get the most from your skating effort without restricting your movement. Stability on skates is not really something that can be taught, but something you acquire through skating often and well.

Both of these elements of skating—balance and stability—equal power. Power provides you with the ability to accelerate quickly and maintain speed and strength throughout the game—and the season. As you move up the hockey ranks, most players will have already learned this lesson. If you want to compete with them you will have to practise hard.

Power skating is simply the ability to use the assets of stability and power to your best advantage to make the most of each and every effort you put into your skating techniques. Your legs will hurt, your chest will burn, but dig in and skate your heart out in learning these skills. They will reward you with a powerful and effective skating style.

Before we end this chapter, let me say that skating is a great form of exercise and can be a source of enjoyment for family and friends, besides forming the most important aspect of the game of hockey.

Don't let your skating skills take a back seat to other skills, for those other skills should be added to well-established skating skills. Only then can they refine your game and add new dimensions to your play.

3 PUCK CONTROL

Hockey, as we've already seen, is a game of many skills whose mastery takes both time and dedication. As skating provides the foundation, puck skills provide the depth and strength in building the total player. Puck control gives the player a chance to reach deep down into a "bag of tricks" and, like a magician who can pull a rabbit from a hat, delight and amaze his audience with quick and dazzling moves. When a seemingly insurmountable obstacle confronts him, he digs deep and, in a flash, is around his startled opponents!

A player's ability to control the puck and enable his team to maintain possession is not only beautiful to watch, but plays a large part in the outcome of most games. Remember, you can't score if you don't have the puck, and the team that controls the puck effectively decreases the opposition's chances to score and increases its own.

After skating, puck control is the most important hockey skill. And, as in skating, you must be comfortable and natural whether you are moving or standing still.

It is important that you learn to keep your balance when you adjust the puck's position in relation to your body. This is not easy, because you must be able to do it without always being able to see the puck. Eventually, you should be able to sense its position at all times without having to look down. It will help if you think of the stick as an extension of your body that receives its instructions through your hand and body movements.

Heads Up It is extremely important when you carry the puck that your head should always be kept up with your eyes looking forward. The player who carries the puck with his head down is "fair game." Since he cannot see where he is going and cannot prepare himself for changes in the game, he leaves himself open to receiving a hard body check when he least expects it or to the embarrassing experience of running into one of his own teammates. Coupled with these obvious drawbacks is the fact that the puck carrier with his head down is in no position to make a pass to a fellow player or to shoot. You can easily see that a player who keeps his head down reduces his effectiveness drastically.

If you skate and carry the puck with your head up, you are able to see not just what is in front of you but also a great deal of what is going on around you. This is commonly referred to as peripheral vision. Your peripheral vision allows you to increase the scope of your vision from the boundary immediately in front of you to your sides in a 180° sweep. Obviously, if you have your chin buried in your chest, your vision is restricted to your feet.

Just one of Wayne Gretzky's great assets is his ability to see all the players on the ice with a single glance and to know without looking sideways exactly where his linemates or defensive partners are situated once they rush into the opponent's zone. This is why he is so often able to give them a perfect pass and put them in the clear for a shot on goal. Ulfie Nilsson, my Swedish centre, also had this uncanny ability. With your head up, you can see what's happening around you and use your peripheral vision to your advantage. Expanding your total awareness of the action on the ice means that you can adjust and react without hesitation.

Carrying the Puck

Before being able to pass and stickhandle effectively, you must learn to carry the puck while moving at high speeds and dodging opposing players. It is an important skill in both your zone and the opposing team's zone, for if you are unable to control the puck effectively, your energies may be spent feverishly chasing the puck about the ice.

When you place the puck in the middle of the stick blade you can either skate with the puck out in front of you—not at your skate tips, which would cause you to lose balance—pushing it ahead of you and skating up to it, or you can skate with the puck on your stick blade at your side, sweeping it along with your forward movement.

Coordination and Comfort To carry the puck effectively you must be able to coordinate your body movements to the constantly changing position of the puck and the puck to the constantly changing position of your body.

Coordination and a feeling of comfort while you're skating with the puck are achieved in two ways. First, you have to learn to position the puck so that you can keep your natural skating rhythm. Do not carry the puck too close to your feet or so far away from your body that you have to stretch to reach it—either position will make you lose your balance and stability. Second, you have to learn to control and move the puck with your stick confidently.

Moving the Puck Around the Opposition As you approach an opposing player, sweep the puck to the side of your body that is away from the opposing player. Do this by cupping your blade around the puck in the direction of the sweep so that you can make your move around him. There are three ways to carry the puck: (1) the one-handed carry, (2) the two-handed carry, and (3) a variation of both.

One-handed carry. In the one-handed carry, guide the puck in front of you with one hand on the butt end of the stick. Move the puck forward by pushing it or manoeuvring it with flicks of the wrist while the blade of your stick is at an angle on the

A forward view of the one-handed carry as I go around Roy.

ice. Then you simply skate to the forward position of the puck.

Two-handed carry. In the two-handed carry, you usually carry the puck in front or to your side with the blade of your stick cupped to protect it. Keep both hands on the stick a comfortable distance apart. Here you skate with the puck closer to your body. You control the puck by sweeping it along with the forward movement of your body.

Variation. The variation is a combination of the one- and two-handed carry. When you approach an opposing player, you can switch the carry to one-handed on one side and protect the puck with your free glove-hand. Or you can come in with a two-handed carry and stickhandle around the defender.

Guarding the Puck Since the object of your opponent is to knock the puck from your control, you must be able to guard it from this attack. You have seen how the variation accomplishes this. Another technique is to sweep the puck to the side of your body that is away from the approaching opponent. Do this by cupping the blade of the stick around the puck in the direction of the sweep so that you can make your move around him.

These explanations describe the art of the forehand carry, but in hockey, direction changes quickly and sometimes with little notice. This is why the forehand carry is supplemented by other techniques.

Carrying the puck, I approach Roy and make my move to the left.

As I switch my weight to the left leg, my body presents less of a target to hit, and I sweep the puck away from Roy.

Roy attempts the check, but it's too late—I'm around him.

With Roy out of the play, I return to a two-handed carry and move in on net alone.

Backhand carry. The backhand carry is executed by positioning the puck on your backhand at the mid-point of the blade. Place your stick in front of the puck, and cradle or cup the blade in the opposite direction to the forehand carry.

To return the puck to the forehand carry, place the stick blade behind the puck.

The full-sweep carry. This manoeuvre is effective when you are standing still and an attacker rushes you. Cup the puck in your stick blade and, as the attacker comes closer, sweep the puck either to the left or right while pivoting on your skates. As you continue through an entire circle with the puck, you draw the attacker to the side of the sweep and before he knows it the puck is now on the other side of your body and you are freely skating forward.

You can do the full-sweep carry on your forehand or your backhand.

It should by now be apparent that the ability to carry the puck effectively is an important aspect of the game. We can now move to one of the more dramatic forms of puck control—stickhandling.

The Art of Stickhandling

Stickhandling is the ability to control the puck by moving it back and forth with your stick so that opponents cannot get possession of it.

Hold your stick with your hands a comfortable distance apart. Keep your grip loose and your wrists flexible. Cup the puck in the curve of the blade and move the puck from one side of your body to the other, back and forth in a smooth, deliberate, sweeping motion. Do this by gently flicking your wrists in the direction you wish to move the puck. To return the puck to its point of origin, place the stick in the puck's path, and at the moment of contact propel it back to the point it started from. Repeat this sequence. When you execute the movement quickly, it appears that the puck is glued to your stick.

Naturally, you should first practise this manoeuvre standing still to gain accuracy, rhythm, and

The start of stickhandling, with the puck cradled in the blade of my stick.

I propel the puck to my right.

I place my stick to the left of my body to await the puck's movement.

I stop the puck's movement on the backhand of the blade.

I return the blade to the forehand, either to start the movement again or to shoot.

speed. Then you can try skating and stickhandling with the puck. Attempt this exercise slowly, without skating variations such as crossovers.

To learn to stickhandle effectively when skating you should, at first, look down to see the position of your body, the puck, and your stick. But this momentary departure from heads-up play is only to give you a feel for the puck and the ability to feel your movement so that you can accommodate your stickhandling to the position of your body when skating forward, sideways, or backwards. The puck should always be far enough away from your body so that it does not get caught up in your feet and cause you to lose momentum and balance or break your skating rhythm.

After you have mastered the ability to skate and stickhandle at the same time, you can add variations. There are three kinds of stickhandling variations: (1) side to side, (2) back and forth, and (3) a diagonal variation of both. Once you have mastered these manoeuvres while standing still, you can practise them while skating forward with your head up. Then do the same skating backwards.

Stickhandling is viewed by some as a lost art in today's style of hockey. This is unfortunate, because it can increase your effectiveness dramatically.

You can learn a lot by watching the great stickhandlers playing today. Keep an eye on the skills of players like Wayne Gretzky, Kent Nilsson, the Stastnys, Guy Lafleur, Gilbert Perrault, Denis Savard, Anders Hedberg, Dale Hawerchuck, and Marcel Dionne.

Watch them manoeuvre the puck and see if you can detect the individual styles that make them so effective. But remember that this skill requires patience and many long hours of practice. Keep working until you can stickhandle perfectly.

Passing

Passing is the art of directing the puck to a teammate in such a way that he gains control of it. Aim at his stick, but if he is moving you should aim the pass to an area in front of him so that he can receive the pass without stopping or slowing down.

Naturally, passes can be intercepted by opposing players, so you should pass only when the receiver is open for a pass and the chances of interception are small. Passing is, however, the best way to move the puck quickly to teammates to improve your team's scoring chances.

Passes are made with both hands on the stick, a comfortable distance apart. Both hands then move in the direction in which the passer intends the puck to move.

The Sweep Pass Practise the sweep pass with another player who is standing approximately ten to fifteen feet away from you. Keep your wrists stiff and move the blade of the stick along the surface of the ice in a consistent sweeping motion. Follow through so that your hands and arms point at the target—your stick blade should point directly at the blade of the receiving player's stick, which serves as the target for your pass. The puck will slide along the ice to the blade of the receiving player's stick.

When you receive a pass, be careful that your stick is not held too firmly, otherwise the puck will jump off the stick blade when the puck hits it. Your

I propel the puck to Roy's stick (presenting a target) as my blade points toward the target.

Roy receives the puck as I complete my follow-through.

grip must be flexible enough to accept the forward movement of the puck in one fluid motion and at the same time allow you to maintain control. When the puck first touches your stick, smoothly move the blade back a foot or two in the same direction the puck is travelling. This will further ensure a soft contact and easy reception. Always try to keep the puck flat on the ice, since rolling or lifted pucks are hard to control.

The misdirected pass. If a pass is aimed badly, you must be prepared to compensate for it. For example, if the pass goes to your feet, either kick the puck forward or turn your skate blade to an angle that will stop the puck and redirect it to your stick.

Receivers, be sure that you provide the passer with a target at all times, just as a baseball catcher does for the pitcher. Passers, if you concentrate, it is just as easy to put the puck on a fellow player's stick as it is to put it to his feet or several yards in front of or behind him.

Passing on the move. The sweep pass becomes more difficult when you pass the puck to a moving player. You must take into account the speed and forward movement of the receiving player's stick and body, and time the pass to your teammate perfectly.

You should perfect the standing pass drill before attempting to pass to a player who is moving. Practise passing to a player on the move in two ways: (1) the passing player stands still and the receiving player skates down the ice to receive the pass, and (2) both players skate and pass the puck back and forth.

Mastery of this drill is extremely important. In hockey, control of the puck through passing is the building block for setting up plays.

Certain hockey teams are labelled as passing teams because their ability to control the puck through passing is one of their outstanding strengths. Others are designated skating teams because individual players can carry the puck into the opposing team's zone not by passing but by skating ability. When the skills of both the skating and passing team combine, a truly exciting, entertaining, well-rounded hockey club is formed. Therefore, it is essential that you practise both skating and puck control drills to develop these skills.

Deking Deking in hockey is identical to a football player moving his head one way and then going in the other direction, or moving his hips one way and going in the opposite direction. This fake is accomplished in the same way in hockey. For example, a player will drop his shoulder and his head to the left and move quickly to the right, bringing the puck to the right side of his body. If the opposing player has been fooled and has moved to the left, he is now at the furthest point away from the puck carrier's stick.

Naturally, this can be done in the opposite direction—the player drops his head and his shoulder to the right, then goes to the left, or uses a double or triple deke by shifting both ways, in an

As Roy races along the boards, I start the pass as I skate with him.

The puck, now midway between us, is sufficiently ahead of Roy to be on target.

Roy receives the pass on the move without either of us losing a stride.

attempt to confuse the defensive player about where he is actually going. These particular dekes require good timing, agility in skating, skillful puck handling, and movements of the body, head, and arms that are accomplished in a quick and deliberate fashion.

Exotic Passes

After you learn how to control the puck and to deke, you might want to try some exotic passes like the flip pass, drop pass, skate pass, slap pass, and others. All of these represent a refinement and extension of the traditional sweep passing method and are extremely effective in mixing up your plays—then you won't become known to the opposing team as a "one-play" player.

All too often, we see players making a move to the left because that is their strong position in skating. Consequently I have emphasized the need for proper skating ability in *all* areas. Once an opposing team becomes aware of a player's weaknesses, that team will attempt to capitalize on those weaknesses as much as possible. It is easy to recognize players who always rely on their strengths. But at the same time they reveal their weaknesses to the other team. It is each player's responsibility to provide himself with well-rounded skills to help his team and heighten his individual contribution in every game.

Flip Pass The flip pass involves lifting the puck over the stick or body of an opposing player so that it lands near your teammate's stick. This is in contrast to the sweep pass, which slides the puck along the surface of the ice.

This type of pass is a difficult one to master because of the timing and touch required to raise the puck high enough to clear obstacles, yet soft enough to land on the other side so that your teammate can make contact. Chico Maki, my teammate in Chicago for many years, was a master at lifting the puck over sticks and fallen opponents, and having it land flat and smooth on my stick as I raced toward the goal.

Remember, you are not shooting the puck, but merely lifting it gently over obstacles. Keep in mind that the puck must land near enough to your teammate's stick so that he can receive the pass and maintain control of the puck without losing momentum or balance. With the flip pass there is always the risk of a rolling puck, which is difficult to handle. However, the benefit of this type of pass far outweighs this risk. The flip pass is truly artis-

tic and can be perfected only through hours of practice.

The flip pass: Roy's stick provides a target, and I gently project the puck over the attacker's stick.

The puck proceeds over the attacker's stick as I aim my follow-through at the target. The puck lands, gently meeting its target, as I complete my follow-through.

Drop Pass When the opposing player has positioned himself in such a way that you can neither get around him nor pass the puck ahead to your teammate, try the drop pass.

As you are carrying the puck, place your stick in front of it. The puck will come to an abrupt stop, and you skate past it. The teammate following behind you picks it up, and your body blocks the opposing player from your teammate and the puck.

With Roy trailing me, I drop the puck between my legs by stopping its movement with the back portion of the blade.

Proceeding forward, I've avoided contact with the puck as Roy picks it up.

This is a tricky pass. If the forward motion of the puck is not stopped when you make contact with the opposing player, the puck will continue forward, and the player trailing behind you will not get it. Remember, the puck's forward motion is stopped by placing your stick blade in front of the puck as you approach the opposing player with the puck between your legs. Do not *pass* the puck backwards (or "put a tail on it"). Make sure it stops dead and that you skate past it and block the oncoming checker. Remember to position your skates so they avoid hitting the dropped puck.

Skate Pass Occasionally, you may find yourself checked so tightly that you cannot use your stick to pass to a teammate who is open. So use your skate to direct the puck to your teammate by kicking it with the side of the blade.

Roy ties me up on the boards. I place my skate blade sideways with the puck in the middle and kick it out sideways toward a teammate.

Practise handling the puck with your skates. During a game a teammate may pass a puck into your feet or you may be able to intercept an errant opposition pass with your skates. Your ability to handle your feet and direct the puck to your stick will give you a big advantage. Watch the European players in the National Hockey League; they all can use their feet to great advantage, a result of their soccer-playing ability. So spend some time kicking the soccer ball around at school, at the playground, and in training. It will definitely enhance your ability to handle the puck with your skates.

Behind-the-Back Pass When you can't pass in front or to the side, the only pass left is around your back. Cup the puck in the blade of your stick and make a smooth sweep on your backhand. Turn your hips and, when you have turned enough, release the puck to your teammate.

As Roy races toward the blue line, I place the puck on my backhand and wrap it around my body, releasing it toward the target.

As the puck proceeds toward its target, note that my follow-through has left the blade of my stick pointing toward the target.

Lead Pass Just as its name indicates, the lead pass is aimed to a point on the ice ahead of its intended receiver. This pass should be used when a direct pass is impossible. Lead passes lead to very fast breaks, but timing and placement are critical to ensure that your teammate receives the puck.

Using the Boards When all else fails, there are always the boards. The boards are an effective tool in passing (1) to another player, (2) to yourself, or (3) around the boards if no one is open.

You will see good players testing the bounce off the boards in practice; this knowledge will be used at game time. As in a bank shot in pool, you must judge the point at which to hit the boards in order to successfully direct the puck in the direction you want it to go.

Give-and-Go Pass The give-and-go pass creates the advantage of a quick and surprising surge of speed—the puck carrier passes the puck to a receiver and then races ahead with a burst of speed to receive a quick return pass from the second player. Opposition players cannot usually react quickly enough to this passing play and often find themselves caught out of position and eliminated from the play.

Bobby Orr excelled at this play. As an opposition checker moved in on him, while he was carrying the puck from behind his own net or out of the corner, he would sharply pass the puck to a teammate in good position. Then he would elude the oncoming checker, burst past him, and receive the puck back from his teammate. This eliminated the checker from the play and left him deep in the opposition's zone. Meanwhile Orr raced up ice to lead plays in the attacking zone. Smart players use this play to avoid a lot of dangerous stickhandling past an opponent (and the possibility of being checked) and a great deal of tiring body contact.

Snap Pass When passes must be executed quickly, use either the snap pass or the slap pass. For the snap pass, position the puck in the curve of the blade and pass the puck with a quick snap of the wrist that brings the palm of the hand up quickly. Increase the accuracy of the pass by pointing the blade to the target.

Slap Pass When a player who has received a pass wants to release the puck quickly to another player, he uses the slap pass. Bring the stick straight back a short distance and then quickly bring the blade forward and strike the puck in a choppy motion. The pass is made quickly but accuracy could be a problem since the passer's initial control is minimal.

Backhand Pass Use the backhand to pass to a teammate on your backhand side. Sweep the puck from the forehand position across your body to the

On the backhand the puck is propelled toward Roy's stick.

My blade now points ahead of Roy's to the position where he is skating.

The puck proceeds on target to his stick as I complete my follow-through.

backhand position. Return the puck across the front of your body with a smooth sweeping backhand pass aimed at the receiving player's stick.

All these passes require a great deal of concentration and practice in order for you to perform them well. Use the photos in this book to help you develop these skills. It will also be very helpful for you to watch opposing players execute the same passes. Learn from their actions and abilities!

These passes can be practised off the ice too.

Naturally, there is a dramatic difference in the speed of the puck on and off the ice surface, but the movements and actions necessary to perform these passes can be practised adequately in street hockey and roller hockey, in back yards and basements.

You must feel completely comfortable and confident with the puck on your stick, and only constant practice will provide that ease and confidence.

To review, skillful puck control will provide you with a bag of tricks that will confuse opposing players and increase your effectiveness when added to your skating skills. But let me emphasize that unless you can skate well in *all* directions, many of these skills cannot be put to use. However, once you feel comfortable with this control over the puck, you are ready to learn how to propel it toward the net with blazing speed and deadly accuracy.

9

4
SHOOTING

The arsenal of the hockey player is strengthened by his ability to shoot the puck in a variety of ways, and the most devastating weapon in this arsenal is the slapshot. Shooting the puck effectively and accurately is a great asset, and if you can combine that with puck control, you will possess a dynamic duo of skills. Whether practising on the ice or off, to master shooting skills, you must pay attention to controlling the puck to gain accuracy, and to learning to take all types of shots quickly and at the right moment.

The steps leading up to taking a shot are very important. The first is deciding whether to shoot at all! This may sound strange, but every time you shoot the puck you run the risk of giving up control, so the choice of when to shoot becomes critical. The SAFETY components should be followed precisely.

At the same time you decide to shoot, you must choose the type of shot to take and place it properly. This strategic placement is called "picking your spot" and translates into the ability of the shooter to pick an opening not protected by the goaltender and shoot to that place. Most often this means picking the corners, but, more important, you must concentrate on hitting the net every time.

Taking the Shot

X Marks the Spot   "Where should I shoot from?" This is a very good question, for you must be able to judge your position on the ice at all times and know whether or not you are in the ideal spot from which to shoot. Equally important is the shooter's ability to know where the net is at all times. Some claim this skill cannot be taught, but a shooter who knows the proper places to shoot from can judge the net's location with amazing accuracy. So it's important to pay attention to learning the best

possible positions on the ice from which to shoot. These positions are determined by the X's that mark the spots, just like buried treasure.

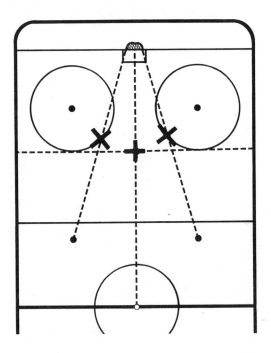

When shooting alleys are drawn from the net, as pictured below, the centre of these alleys mark the ideal shooting slots. These positions give the shooter a clear and direct path to the goal without reducing the amount of net to shoot at because of a poor shooting angle. (The great Maurice "The Rocket" Richard used to contend that a shot on net was a potential goal, and he would shoot from anywhere in the attacking zone and still score goals for his team, the Montreal Canadiens.)

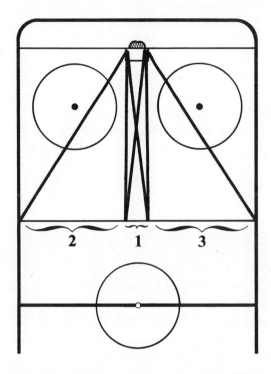

The Shooter's Curve The shooting positions are numbered from best (1) to worst (5) on the shooting curve below.

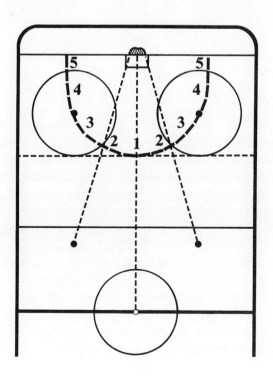

As the shooter moves to a higher number on the curve, the area of the net he has to shoot at (pictured by the triangles) decreases, thereby reducing his chance of scoring. Obviously, the player who continually carries the puck to the outside automatically reduces his own opportunity for a shot.

A puck carrier who carries the puck wide of a defender and to the outside will draw the defender with him. This will enable a teammate to skate into the area vacated by the defender. With a good accurate pass from the outside or corner area the puck carrier can provide a teammate with a good chance on goal from one of the danger areas marked with an X.

A *thinking* hockey player who skates with these diagrams in mind quickly learns to use them to increase his scoring chances and score more goals. Remember—X marks the spot!

The Shooter's Triangle When you are going to shoot, you must be aware of the triangle that is formed by your body and the two goalposts. Your awareness of this triangle will give you an additional edge in evaluating your position and the amount of net available to shoot at.

This awareness will also help you make the decision to shoot, pass, or carry. Becoming familiar with the zones you cover is extremely important in helping you make the split-second decisions required of you and react to the decisions a teammate makes.

After the Shot Your responsibility does not end with taking the shot. Once the shot is released, you should proceed as quickly as possible in its direction to be in position to play any rebounds, regain possession of the puck, or take a second shot. This type of alert reaction keeps you in the play and affords you the obvious opportunity of reducing the possibility of losing possession of the puck. Remember, every time you shoot, you are faced with this possible loss. Your ability to react quickly aids in reducing the chance of error.

Control and Accuracy Speed, direction, and height of shots must be controlled. The situation in which the shot is taken dictates the vital importance of these three factors.

Accuracy simply means that you must be able to propel the puck where you want it to go with precision. Picking corners is important, but it is also important, each time you shoot, to make sure the puck hits the net. Any shot directed at this area is a potential goal. If your shot is not accurate, you will have no chance to score and every chance of losing possession.

Speed. The shot's speed is controlled by the degree of snap in your wrists, arms, and upper body; the amount of body weight used to compress the shaft of your stick; and the coordination of these elements as you move in the direction of the shot.

Direction. You control the direction of your shot by a proper follow-through and by exerting control over your wrist and body movement when taking the shot.

Height. The elevation of the puck is determined by the snap of the wrists and arms and the height of your follow-through. More snap in the arms and wrists and a higher follow-through will cause the puck to rise higher. A lower follow-through and a more subdued snapping motion will keep the puck lower.

Shooting

The Best Shot The best possible shot in hockey, most experts agree, is one that is low to the ice, maybe two to four inches off the ice surface. This shot is the one most goaltenders dread. A low shot lands at the goaltender's feet, and is the most difficult shot for him to stop, especially if he is constantly moving up and down to make saves. It also allows your teammate to deflect the puck past the goalie. A higher shot can be seen more readily and can be stopped by the big knock-down glove or the catching mitt, making it much easier for the goaltender to stop the puck. So, develop a shot in which the puck either skims across the ice, or one that keeps it within six inches of the ice.

Controlling the Puck Keeping the puck down when attempting to take the slap shot or any other shot is not an easy task. But practice will help you adjust the level of your shots.

Normally, if you keep the puck in the middle to front of the blade, keep both hands firmly gripped, snap your wrist quickly and keep your follow-through low, the puck should rise only a few inches off the ice. If you place your stick blade at an angle other than the fully cupped position and use a higher follow-through, your shot will rise higher.

Naturally, there will be times when the puck must be lifted over the goaltender or raised to a high corner that is left exposed. This is accom-

plished by a more accentuated snapping of the wrist and a more abrupt and higher follow-through toward your target—the upper part of the net.

Accuracy in directing the shot to the net is also difficult. Anyone who has served a tennis ball can attest to the fact that it requires a great deal of concentration and training to hit the right spot consistently. The same is true for hockey.

The slap shot especially, because the fast and complicated movements required to shoot it make its route unpredictable, and because the player is attempting to shoot the puck as hard as possible, is hard to shoot accurately. Very few players can put the puck right where they want to with a slap shot, and some players will openly admit that they just shoot the puck as hard as possible toward the net and hope that it goes directly in, or hits a player and deflects in or is tipped in.

But if you cannot effectively put the puck on the net with a slap shot and you continually miss the net, you deprive your team of scoring chances and cause them to lose control of the puck. The player who is able to attain control over his shots is the player who will score time after time. There are other shots that can be controlled better and that will hit the net more frequently. These must also become a part of the hockey player's arsenal.

The Slap Shot The slap shot is one of the most attractive and effective shots used in hockey today. Its unpredictable path leaves the goaltender at the shooter's mercy. Although the shooter's lack of full control obviously benefits the goaltender somewhat, the speed of the slap shot favours the shooter, and the goaltender is at a further disadvantage because he does not know exactly where to look for the shot to explode from the shooter's stick.

The slap shot can be a great weapon—if used properly and at the right time. Not only are many goals scored by the slap shot, but also many plays resulting in goals begin with a slap shot. For example, a defender might commit himself by going down on a one-knee or two-knee block or might sprawl in front of the shooter. The committed player has put himself out of the play and the shooter might manoeuvre around him and make a pass that results in a goal from close range.

To slap the puck well you must have good balance and timing. Timing, especially when you are moving, is of utmost importance in obtaining the proper speed and direction of the shot. You must

The slap shot: the back (pendulum) swing as it begins its downward movement, with the puck in the middle of the legs, weight evenly distributed, front knee slightly bent, and eyes on the puck.

Halfway down the pendulum, your shoulders are square, your eyes are on the puck, and the weight shifts forward as the rear leg leaves the ice.

Contact is made. The shaft is compressed, and your eyes are now on the target, as the back leg is swung.

The follow-through points at the target, with the body's entire weight now forward.

know where to distribute your weight and which leg to shoot off. You must know when to push the puck in front of you, when to raise your stick, and the exact moment to get the puck away without having it blocked or deflected by a defender.

You also need a stick stiff enough in the blade and shaft to be able to withstand the force of the stick striking the ice and puck at the same time. If the blade of the stick is weak or flimsy, the force of the contact by the stick blade will cause the blade to give way to the force. The puck will not spring from the blade and will fail to project directly in the line of your follow-through. Instead it will act like a slice from a golf club and go limply left or right of your target, depending on whether you are a right- or left-hand shooter. The stiffness of the shaft of your stick also may have much the same effect on your shot. If the shaft is too flimsy, then the same force on contact will cause it to spring away from your energy force. It will fail to return to its normal position, and the puck will leave the stick blade feebly and fail to go where you want it to. All the energy you have put into the downswing and follow-through will be wasted. So make sure you have a stick stiff enough to act as a proper tool for all the weight, force, and energy you will put into your shot.

If you are a left-hand shooter, begin your slap shot by pushing the puck out in front of you a comfortable distance (with constant practice you will be able to judge this distance). Raise your stick in a sharp upward motion past your left side and above your head. Slide your left hand down the shaft a comfortable distance. This will depend on the length of your stick, your height, and your skating style. Your body will coil as you catch up to the puck and your hands and arms should start downward in a rapid motion with the stick blade targeted on the puck, which is now at your side and slightly ahead of you.

At the point where the stick blade, the ice, and the puck meet your body will uncoil with all your weight now on your right foot and your left hand gripped tightly on the shaft of the stick. The tight grip on the bottom hand is very, very important to the execution. At contact, your left foot will swing off the ice and behind the right leg. This will balance you as your hands and arms snap violently in the direction of the shot. If you wish the puck to take a high trajectory, follow through completely with your hands, arms, and stick. Conversely, if you want a low shot, follow through on a lower level.

Imagine a puck hurtling at almost 120 miles per hour toward the net. The goaltender, with an array of players in front of his net, must try to see the puck at all times and then stop it. No wonder the slap shot is a goaltender's nightmare!

Variations of the slap shot. Variations of the slap shot are used when there is not enough space or time for a full shot. These shots are ones in which you cut down on the actual pendulum swing. Obviously, the most effective and devastating shot is one in which you are in full stride and can take a full pendulum swing. Although shots that are taken at different levels of swing can be effective, they lose the speed that often catches the goaltender off guard. During power plays and when players stand in front of the opposing team's goalie to block his vision ("screening" him), the slap shot, kept low to the ice, is most effective.

The Wrist Shot The wrist shot is an effective method of shooting the puck with a great degree of accuracy and speed, but without the full swing movement of the slap shot. The wrist shot obtains its speed from the strength of the player's wrist, arms, and upper body. The most used and most important shot to master, the wrist shot scores most of the goals in any league—from minor mites to the NHL. In order to be able to wrist the puck well, you need balance and timing.

You might wonder how Mike Bossy of the New York Islanders gets the puck away so quickly and accurately with such great force in such a blur of motion. Well, in order for Mike to do so, he must have mentally taken the wrist shot before he receives the puck. After positioning properly for the

shot, all the fundamentals that go into shooting the wrist shot have been completed in his mind: (1) the target has been surveyed, (2) the puck has already been received and is in good position and controlled by the stick blade, (3) his hands and wrists have been cocked, and (4) his balance is distributed evenly over and slightly behind the puck.

If you have run through this procedure rapidly in your mind in preparation for a wrist shot, all that's left to do when you actually receive the puck is to (1) place your weight on the stick shaft, (2) cup your blade over the puck, (3) snap your wrist and forearms, putting all your weight on your stick shaft behind the shot, and (4) follow through with a rapid transfer of your body weight.

The height of the shot will again depend on the height of your follow-through. A high follow-through of your hands and arms will fling the puck high; a low follow-through will keep the puck low.

It is very important to time exactly when to lay your weight on the shaft of your stick and drag it through to the point of release, when to snap your hands and wrists, and when to throw your entire body weight behind the shot. Only then will you get the maximum power and velocity in your shots. A wrist shot can travel almost 100 miles per hour, so you can imagine the havoc that forwards visit on opposing goaltenders, especially at close range.

In the wrist shot, the blade of the stick is always in contact with the puck and never leaves the ice. Therefore, the player has maximum control of the puck and can wait until the last moment to release it. This amount of control allows for a better op-

With the puck on the forehand and the blade on the ice, place your weight on the left leg as the right leg leaves the ice. Keep your eyes on the puck.

44

Cup the blade around the puck as you shift your weight forward and your eyes to the target.

The stick shaft is compressed, and your weight is fully forward on one leg.

The puck is released. Eyes are on the target and the knee is bent. Follow through with the blade pointing at the target as the wrists and arms are snapped.

portunity to shoot the puck accurately on the net, and also allows the player to alter his shot quickly if he realizes that a pass would create a better scoring chance.

The Sweep Shot In a fast game like hockey, sometimes situations arise where the puck must be shot in one fluid movement without the slightest hesitation. The sweep shot handles this situation best. This is especially true when a pass is sent with no time to stop it to prepare for the shot. Keep the stick blade on the ice, and cup the puck with the blade. Send the puck toward the net in a smooth sweeping motion using the weight of your body. Keep your legs a shoulder width apart. As you make contact with the puck, cradle it in the curve of your blade as your body weight shifts from the rear leg to the front leg. Aim your follow-through at the net.

Naturally, when the puck is passed to you, you must time the sweeping movement of your stick so that it meets the puck and propels it in the direction of the net in one unbroken motion.

The Backhand Shot When you are not able to shoot on your forehand because of opposing players attempting to intercept the puck, you should know how to take a backhand shot. To illustrate the necessity for the backhand shot, picture a situation where a right-handed player is skating toward an opposing player. He then turns sharply to the left away from the net. The puck would be in a position on his stick where it could only be shot toward the net on the back hand or back portion of the stick blade.

There are some who contend that the curved stick used today affects the backhand shot. Basically there is no real truth to this, since most good hockey players have been able to handle both the forehand and the backhand shots effectively with the curved blade of the hockey stick.

The backhand shot is accomplished by placing the puck in the middle or the heel of the back portion of the stick blade. The velocity and lifting power of the shot comes from moving the blade of the stick along the ice in the direction of the target and flinging the puck off the stick in a sweeping motion. The backhand shot does not carry nearly the same force and effectiveness as the wrist and slap shot mainly because it is practised less, and your muscle formation supplies less power in a backward motion compared to the more natural forward motion; as well, the curved blades cut

The puck is on my backhand and my eyes are on the puck, with the stick blade approaching Sal.

I sweep my arms in the direction of the net with my follow-through pointing toward the net as I release the puck.

down the blade area available at right angles to the puck.

But in those situations where the player's body is placed in a position that will not allow a forehand shot, the only alternative is to proceed with the backhand in order to get the puck on the net. This is especially true when the puck carrier approaches the opposition goal from his off wing and a defender prevents the shooter from getting his body, his stick, and the puck in a position to shoot from the forehand. Anders Hedberg has a very accurate backhand and gets it away quickly while moving in on the right wing, since he is a left-handed shooter.

Mastering the backhand shot, as with any other technique in hockey, requires a lot of practice and exercise. Building strength in the arms and wrists will help you achieve crisp and accurate shots.

The Snap Shot When shots must be taken quickly, some shooters choose to take what is referred to as a snap shot, a variation of the wrist shot. Compared with other shots, its speed and accuracy are average. Hit the puck with a short snapping motion and aim it toward the net. The snap shot is not like a slap shot even though the stick is drawn back from the puck before striking it. It has more of the characteristics of a wrist shot because of the body weight applied to the stick, compressing it on contact, and the tremendous snap of the wrists, arms, and upper body on contact with the puck. As with all shots, the follow-through determines the height of the shot.

The snap shot: as I approach the net, the blade is on the ice and my eyes are on the target.

I bring the blade back slightly, off the ice and away from the puck. My weight is on my left leg.

Facing the net squarely, I snap my wrists and arms as my back leg leaves the ice, placing my weight forward.

When the wrists are snapped, the follow-through points toward the net.

The Screen Shot and the Deflection A screen shot needs two players: the player taking the shot and a second player who stands in front of the opposing team's net and, without entering the goaltender's crease, screens the goaltender—blocks the goaltender's line of sight in order to let the shooter aim at an open spot. As the puck moves toward the net, the screening player can either let the puck pass him or he can attempt to deflect it with his stick or body. (He cannot deliberately touch it with his skate, because a puck kicked into the net does not count as a goal.) The sudden change in the puck's direction caused by a deflection confuses the goalie and reduces his ability to react quickly and make the save.

You might think that facing slap shots, wrist shots and all their variations would be agony

enough for a goaltender, but the deflection is a real horror. Not only can its unpredictability leave a goaltender helpless against making the save, but the same unpredictability can also cause an injury—two reasons why you will see defencemen feverishly trying to move opponents away from the front of the net.

Roy shoots the puck toward the net as I move into position, with Sal reacting to the shot.

As the puck comes near my stick, I deflect it toward the net over Sal's pad.

As I skate in on Roy he screens (blocks) Sal's view, and I release the puck through his legs. Note how Sal has to look around Roy to see me, putting him off balance.

47

Fake Shot Reacting to certain situations with an open mind can create better alternatives. For example, when you wind up to take a shot, sometimes the defending player will commit himself and make a move in anticipation of the shot. This will give you another alternative besides shooting that you did not have before your opponent's commitment.

A smart player will be able to fake a shot, force the defender to make his move, and, in a split second, take advantage of this move—not to shoot, but to go around the man.

Shooter's Judgement

All shots must be used with discretion. The shooter who uses good judgement and who makes decisions quickly and properly becomes what is called a "smart hockey player." This implies that he does not use only slap or wrist shots in every instance, without any change. He has the sense to pick a shot to meet the exact needs of the situation.

Hockey is a thinking person's game, and you must be prepared, and aware of your actions on the ice. You cannot simply go through the motions and expect to play the game well. To be successful you must concentrate, and be continually aware of your actions and the actions of the opposing players.

Better Position The ability to reposition yourself will in most instances place you in a better position to shoot. Naturally, you make a move to go around your opponent because your shot from that position may not be the best one available. But let me remind you again that if you have a good shot, take it! Don't give up an opportunity, then try to make another one. The decision to shoot, pass, or carry is an important one that demands exact and precise judgement.

Variations Every player should know how to take all these shots and a good player will use *all* of them to become a productive goal scorer and to confuse the opposition. It would be fruitless to take the same shot again and again and have the goaltender be prepared each time. If you can mix up your shots and use the right type of shot at the right time, you will become a consistent goal scorer and also maintain control of the puck for your team.

Of course, no player masters all the skills for every aspect of the sport, but every player can play well and be a useful addition to any team. It is reasonable to expect that every player have a designated role and a strength that can contribute toward playing the game well and having fun.

For very young hockey players, it is extremely important that each child get a chance to play and that coaches forget about winning for winning's sake and think of the child having fun and developing, both physically and emotionally, as a result of playing the sport. In the later years of a player's hockey career, winning and team play become essential components of competition, and this is good because strong competition teaches a player to perform with a high degree of skill and to learn to accept the pain of defeat that is inevitable for all players in sports.

9

FLIP-A-SKILL

An Explanation of Flip-a-Skill

Each Flip-a-Skill sequence consists of 32 single-frame photographs in order. When you flip the pages of the text, you cause the photos on the page to move the figures in the pictures.

Flip-a-Skill can be used to help overcome the confusion you experience when you attempt to execute a skill while only having at your fingertips a technical text and photographs that show only a portion of the required moves.

Through the magic of Flip-a-Skill you can actually see the entire sequence of moves needed to perform a skill. You can control this movement by the speed at which you flip the pages, and can also stop the action at any time and view a single frame to investigate a positioning movement.

These sequences explain six important skills—forward skating, the one-on-one, forward skating pivot to backward skating, stickhandling, the slap shot, and the wrist shot.

How to Use Flip-a-Skill

1. To view Sequences 1–3, hold the spine of the book in your left hand and the outside edge with your right.
2. Flip the pages from front to back with your right thumb. As you reach the appropriate section, you can see the skill in sequence.
3. To view Sequences 4–6 (on the back of Sequences 1–3), just reverse the procedure: hold the spine of the book with your right hand and flip the pages from back to front with your left thumb.

9

Forward Skating

Executed while carrying the puck (alternating two-handed and one-handed carry) moving up the ice out of the defensive zone.

The One-on-One

The classic confrontation, featuring: forward skating with crossovers, one- and two-handed carry, deke, going around defencemen, skating backwards (playing the oncoming attacker), and a wrist shot on net.

Forward Skating Pivot to Backward Skating

Execution of this movement, with alternating backward crossovers.

The Art of Stickhandling

Performed while skating forward, adjusting the puck's position, and alternating the distribution of weight (with the puck carrier's head up).

The Slapshot

Showing the approach, setup, execution, and follow-through of the shot.

The Wrist Shot

Featuring the approach on the goaltender, the goaltender playing the angle, the wrist shot, the attempted save, and the score.

5 OFFENSIVE PLAY

A sustained attempt to score a goal raises fans to their feet and heightens the excitement of the game. The sensation created by a team's quick break from their end of the ice with crisp passes and fast skating is a beautiful sight, and the anticipation of a goal increases with each stride toward the net. This coordinated team play, usually orchestrated by a defenceman, is no accident, but the result of hours of practice and the uncanny sixth sense of each player knowing where his fellow players are on the ice without actually seeing them. Offensive play brings together the skills of skating, shooting, and puck control to produce some of the most dramatic moments in sports. For, as the flick of a wrist sends the cords of the net bulging, the red light glows and the siren screams to signal the climactic success that causes pandemonium and tremendous satisfaction... a goal.

Offensive play brings together all the skills you've learned so far for the purpose of scoring a goal, or helping to set one up. If you have worked hard and developed your skills, this is where it is going to pay off.

All too often, players feel that complicated, fancy plays are required to win hockey games. If you watch closely, however, you will see that it is not really the fancy plays that make the difference. It is the team that better executes the basic fundamentals of the game—skating, thinking, positioning, passing, and shooting—that will have an edge over another team.

Fancy plays and those delightful "dipsy doodles" do come in handy in sticky situations, but a really close look will show that they're only the refinement of a basic skill or combination of skills we've learned.

Possession

Hockey is a game of possession—you can't score if you don't have the puck! But, strangely, some teams neglect this simple fact and still scratch their heads after a discouraging loss.

Faceoffs A sure-fire method of obtaining possession of the puck is by winning faceoffs. Faceoffs follow each stoppage of play and are hockey's

The faceoff. Blades point at each other on the edge of the circle. Eyes are fixed with total concentration as the goaltender stands ready.

As the puck is dropped I sweep Roy's stick away from it . . .

. . . and proceed to skate forward toward it.

With Roy out of the play, I use my skates to move the puck forward so that I can carry it up ice.

mechanism to get the game rolling again.

The centres (or other designated players) of the two teams face each other at the faceoff circle, stick blades on the ice pointing at each other. The puck is dropped by the referee or linesman between the centres. As a centre, your aim is to get the puck to a teammate beside you or behind you, or just to tie up the opposing centre so that your teammates can skate into the faceoff area and capture the loose puck.

As the puck is dropped, you must time perfectly the sweep of your stick to sweep it away from the faceoff area to your teammates. To accomplish this you must keep your eye on the puck at all times and balance yourself perfectly so that stability and stick strength are not lost or lessened by poor positioning. Stan Mikita, my teammate for many years in Chicago (and with the St. Catharines Tee-Pees), was one of the best and most consistent winners of faceoffs—and I'm sure Stan will tell you that concentration was a big part of his success.

The centre who can win faceoffs consistently will provide his team with dramatically increased control of the puck. So, practice winning those faceoffs until it becomes second nature.

Shots from the faceoff. Once you've become adroit at winning faceoffs, you can learn to take a shot from the faceoff, when the faceoff occurs to the side of the opposing goaltender.

I remember once in an overtime game in Chicago against the New York Rangers, Pit Martin won the draw to the right of Eddie Giacomin, the New York goaltender. Pit dropped the puck back to me in the slot area, and before Giacomin could move we had won the game.

This play requires skill and can only be done when the timing is perfect. If you miss the shot, which is a single-motion sweep, nine times out of ten you will lose possession of the puck.

Basics All too often, when basic skills are not a mainstay of a team's method of play, possession of the puck is reduced dramatically and, of course, so is the opportunity to score.

Some teams literally give the puck away through mistakes such as (1) shooting desperately when there is no chance to score, (2) passing to a covered player, (3) continually shooting the puck into the opposing end, (4) having no set plays and no communication between linemates, (5) taking foolish penalties, and (6) not refining their skills and not executing the skills they do have.

To help his team keep possession of the puck, each player must know his position well by being aware of (1) the responsibilities of the position, (2) the territorial limitations it presents, (3) the best way to use his skills in the position, and (4) the way to compensate for his weaknesses.

This brings us to how an offensive play actually starts. Let's follow the play as it forms and the changes that take place in each zone as it moves up the ice.

Getting the Puck Out of Your Zone

When you gain possession of the puck in your zone, if you can't get it out quickly and easily, you're in big trouble. This is the time when a properly executed basic play and a little common sense pay off. It is surprising how many teams remain unnecessarily bottled up in their own end of the ice. Sometimes this is due to hesitation.

Hesitation can cause scoring opportunities to evaporate before your eyes and open players to become covered. You must be alert to take advantage of opportunities as they arise, or be able to create your own opportunities through heads-up play. It is important that you know where your teammates and opposition players are even before you get the puck, so that when you do get it, you know where the openings are and what teammate is the right one to pass to. A team should have several set plays to perform in this situation.

The Setup   You must set up a play to have it work properly, and coming out of your own end is best set up by first going behind your net with the puck. Organize yourself, and allow your team to get in place as the wingers come back down the ice and get in position for a breakout pass. Then move out. Remember, you and your teammates must move around to become open for passes. If you stand still, you can be covered easily and your breakout plays will fail. Many hockey experts believe that the player without the puck is as important as the player with the puck, because it is he who must dart into open areas to provide a target for the passer.

The Decision   When you are behind the net you have three options available to you—pass to a winger, pass to your defensive partner, or carry the puck out yourself. The opposing team's formation will tell you which is best, if you are able to read their coverage. Remember, if you carry the puck yourself, a player must cover your position for you. Once your pass is completed, you should move up and assume your proper position.

Timing is critical in executing plays. Swift execution is vital once the decision is made. I emphasize *once the decision is made* because quick release of the puck every time you receive it is an error. You should take as much time to make the decision as is available, to assure complete and proper execution.

Holding the puck until a play appears requires alertness, patience, and concentration. For example, when a defenceman gains possession of the puck in his zone, the forward forechecking might sense or expect a pass up the boards and react by turning away from the defenceman *before* the pass. The smart defenceman who is patient enough to wait has gained an edge. He did not fall prey to the common error of releasing the puck the minute someone covered him, and has increased the ways in which he can move the puck out of his zone.

The best way to move the puck ahead quickly is to *headman the puck*, that is, to pass the puck to a player ahead of you who is not covered by an opposing player. Move the puck quickly before it becomes a desperation attempt, even if it is to a teammate only a few feet from you. If no one is open, it is best to carry the puck yourself as far as possible until a teammate becomes free. Headmanning the puck with accurate, crisp passes to open players can quickly move it up ice.

As I am back in the zone, I pass it up to Roy.

117

Roy receives the puck as he shoots out of the zone.

Be cautious. Some of the most finely executed plays sometimes fail. Players should not advance from their defensive zone until they are sure the puck will be taken out of the zone successfully. If the puck carrier remains in the zone alone, he may be stranded with checkers all over him and no one to pass to. Leaving your own zone too quickly will also leave your team open to a breakaway if an opposing player steals the puck and there is no defenceman between him and the goaltender.

The Neutral Zone

Once you have successfully eliminated the possibility of being trapped in your own zone, you can approach the other team's zone and form plays to penetrate their defence. The neutral zone plays an important part in forming these plays.

While in the neutral zone, it is important that the best puck carrier and playmaker be in control of the puck and that all the forward players try to become open by speeding up or slowing down, cutting across or behind, and performing many more manoeuvres before entering the offensive zone.

The Unbalanced Wedge Basic positional play dictates the outcome of many hockey games, and it is important that the player have a feel for his position on the ice at all times. To illustrate this effectively and to portray the change from defence to offence, let's look at a basic play known as the unbalanced wedge.

The following illustration shows some basic positional responsibilities of the players as they pass from the defensive zone through the neutral zone and deep into the offensive zone.

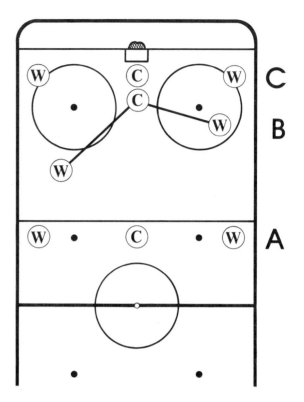

As the three forwards move up and down the ice the wedge (shown in **B**) becomes unbalanced on one side, and changes its form to reflect the position of the players. Naturally, the location of the puck requires players to shift their positions. When this happens, it is important that another player cover any open position. If the player fails to do so the uncovered position gives the opposing team an advantage.

If players enter the offensive zone three across in a straight line (as in **A**), the defensive pair can easily defend against them. For example, a pass across the ice to a teammate can easily be broken up by a defenceman simply sticking his stick out.

The alignment shown in **C**, where all three forwards end up parallel to each other near the goal, should also be avoided. This is the classic example of getting caught too deep in the opposing zone.

Let's have a closer look at the position shown in **B**.

Two in–one out. It is important to examine each player's role in the offensive position. This is best done through the unbalanced-wedge illustrations that follow.

Unbalanced wedge to right.

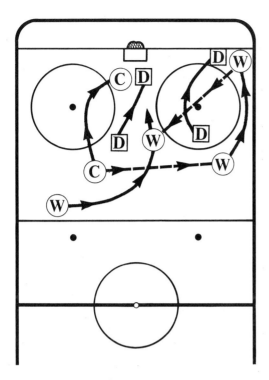

Unbalanced wedge to left.

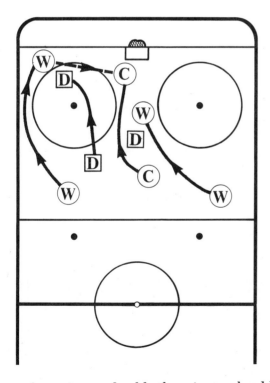

The puck carrier, preferably the winger, should be given the puck in time to get good control as he enters the zone. He should then drive outside, taking the defenceman on that side wide and deep with him.

At the same time, the player in the centre should head for the front of the net area, taking the other

defenceman with him. The third player should swing into the centre, coming into the slot area late to accept a pass from the puck carrier driving wide. If the second defenceman does not go with the player driving for the net, then an option would be for the wide puck carrier to give a pass to the centre in front of the net.

It is important to fix in your mind your position on the wedge and use it as a guide to set the territorial limits of your position.

As seen in the diagrams, the players assume a two-in – one-out formation, an alignment that protects against getting caught too deep in the opposing zone by having one man back ready to check in case the opposing team gets a fast break.

Any player moving from his position on the wedge must have someone cover his place, or else a weakness on that side will result, creating an opening through which the opposing team can quickly get out of its end.

The unbalanced wedge is a basic play that always gives defencemen fits. One defenceman must go after the puck carrier going wide. If he doesn't, the puck carrier can cut around him and head for the net. The other defenceman must pay attention to the second man rushing for the net area. This should leave the slot area open for the third member of the line to move in for a pass and often a shot on goal.

Other Options When approaching the blue line, the puck carrier has several other options at his disposal. He can: (1) pass to a forward, either a lead pass over the blue line or a "give-and-go" before entering the zone, (2) carry the puck in and pass to a forward near the net or drop the puck back to set up a screen shot, (3) shoot the puck in off the boards, or (4) pass back to a defenceman to set up again, if no play is available.

The following diagrams illustrate the different plays for getting the puck across the blue line.

1. Blue-line pass to winger.

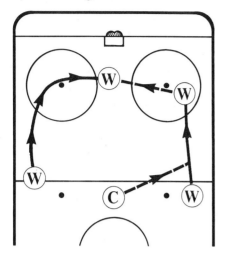

2. Give-and-go.

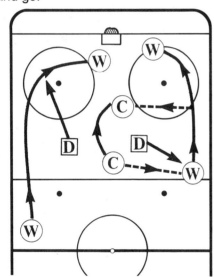

3. Carry in and pass.

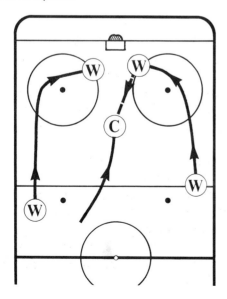

4. Drop pass or screen shot.

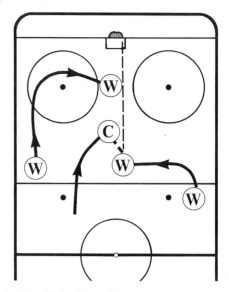

5. Shooting in off the boards.

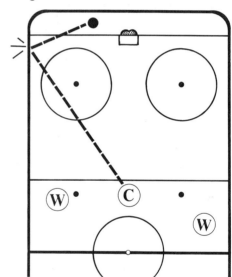

6. Pass back to defenceman.

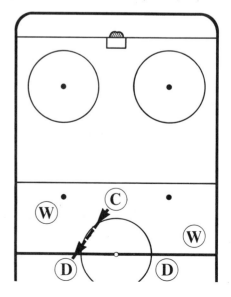

The obvious advantage of plays 1, 2, and 3 is that your team has crossed the opposing team's blue line as a team and is positioned in their zone for rebounds to regain possession or forecheck. And number 6 at least provides you with a chance at setting up a second play and maintaining possession.

The disadvantage created by 4 and 5 is that when you have made either of these plays you have effectively given up possession without a fight, since in 4 the goaltender gains possession if he saves your shot, and in 5 the puck simply goes into a corner rather than to a designated player. This last option should be used only as a last resort, since very few teams possess players who can consistently dig the puck from the boards and regain possession of it. This is a play that requires fast skaters and fearless checkers, though a team that can master the play will increase its possession time dramatically and neutralize the opposing team's chances of setting up their offensive plays.

If you can effectively master all these plays, using each at the proper time, you will be an offensive threat.

Plays in the Offensive Zone

Once you have successfully entered the opposing team's zone and you control the puck there, you must abandon the wedge that got you there. One of the best setups to use is the following:

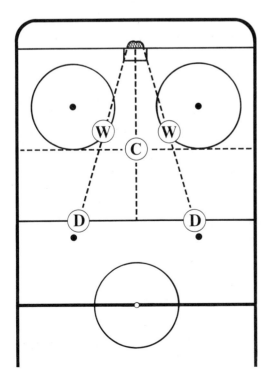

If you draw straight lines to connect the five positions, you will draw four triangles. These triangles represent passing lines for moving the puck closer to the net for a clear shot. Your aim should be to move the puck into one of the ideal shooting spots that were outlined in Chapter 4 (page 41), and then to shoot.

If we superimpose the shooter's curve on the shooting alley diagram where "X marks the spot," you can easily see the areas within which you can move to set up the best shots. Etch these positions in your mind so that reaching them on the ice will trigger an automatic reaction—shoot or pass.

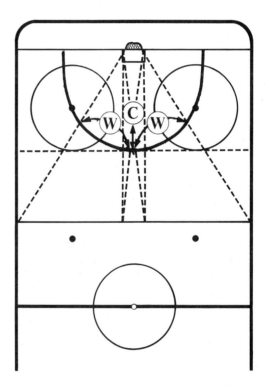

Using The Point Your two defencemen positioned at the opposing team's blue line are called the point. Pass the puck back to the point when you don't have a good shot on net, and then concentrate your efforts around the net area to deflect, screen, or tip in shots from the defencemen. Get in a position to put in any rebounds from the goaltender's saves too.

The point men must shoot the puck past any oncoming checkers and not into their bodies, which would block the puck and perhaps bounce it back past the defencemen. This would neutralize a good play and might even catch your three forwards "in deep" as opposition players pick up the loose puck and break away with only one defender back.

The Power Play

A team that can successfully execute certain set plays or variations of them is a team that will increase its scoring opportunities. The Soviet teams practise the same plays thousands of times so that each play becomes second nature for everyone. One of the most important plays for any team is the power play.

The power play is designed to take advantage of a penalty (or penalties) against the opposing team that leaves them short-handed. It's amazing how some teams cannot mount a sustained attack even while they have more players on the ice.

A good power play is also an important weapon against coaches who encourage their players to intimidate opponents. Once the intimidating team is scored upon consistently, they soon resort to playing within the rules, since the power play causes them to play catch-up hockey.

If your team has either a one-man or two-man advantage against the penalized team, it is important to get the puck to the uncovered player on your team. Some coaches will increase their chances by replacing a defenceman with a forward who can shoot the puck accurately on the net from the point, or make good plays from a defenceman's position.

In the power play, your object is to work the puck close to the net to come into the shooting zone described in Chapter 4 (page 41). Once you have positioned yourself in one of these slots, shoot the puck without wasting any time. A team that continually passes without taking a shot or that hesitates to shoot will see their power play dwindle away rapidly. Passing scores no goals, although clever passing represents the foreplay to a goal.

The normal setup (see page 85) is used to break out of your zone, which is important since you want to get out quickly and cleanly. With the opposing team one player short, you should have no problem! When you skate into the neutral zone, remember that this is where you should spend time setting up the play, since you should have some additional time with the open man provided by the penalty.

Yet this is where most teams panic. If they are fortunate enough to get out of their zone without breaking up the setup, the panic is caused by players who do not stick to their position, but attempt to seize single-handedly the scoring opportunity. The unfortunate result of this is usually broken plays—not goals.

Teams who have good power plays are Boston, Montreal, and Quebec. In the early 1970s, Phil Esposito was the best in the slot or in front of the net, while Ken Hodge, Wayne Cashman, and John Bucyk could dig the puck out of the corners to make plays on the power play. Some of the best all-time playmakers in this situation were John Bucyk, Bert Olmstead, and Dickie Moore. Today's best power playmakers are Bryan Trottier and Wayne Gretzky.

Broken Plays When you lose possession on the power play, it is important that you regroup and set up again. Otherwise, your play will be disorganized and will frustrate and limit your efforts.

Since the power play is a temporary advantage, use set lines and apply continuous pressure. When the opposing team has the puck, two players should constantly follow the puck—one to take the man, the other to take the puck. The team that can relentlessly apply pressure is going to succeed, and all players on the power play must work together as a team to bring about the best opportunity to score.

The Fast Break

Sometimes plays are formed that are a direct result of players' leaving their positions. You must know where your teammates are going to be to take advantage of these formations. The ability to capitalize on situations brought about by fast breaks is vital in adding that refined touch to offensive play. Some of these situations are:

The three-on-two. When forwards are caught deep in the opposing team's zone or don't backcheck, the opposing forwards can find themselves with the puck and with only two opposing defencemen back to defend.

As the three forwards come across the blue line, the two defencemen cannot commit themselves because they are outnumbered. This allows the forwards the advantage of *backing them up* into their own zone. Each line on the team should have plays that they practise in order to take advantage of this situation.

The two-on-one. The two-on-one play is relatively easy to execute. One player attempts to draw the lone defenceman to him and then pass to his teammate, who is all alone in front of the net.

The three-on-one. The three-on-one situation also leaves the defenceman at the forward's mercy. You have many more possibilities for scoring than with a two-on-one.

The Breakaway When everyone is playing at one end, a quick pass or a missed puck can result in the dynamic play of a skater going in alone on the goaltender. This play usually brings the fans to their feet in anticipation of the score or in the hope of the save. The shooter naturally uses the play best suited for him—a shot or a deke and fake.

But remember, you must seize these opportunities and use them to your advantage. An alert and thinking hockey club will capitalize on them without hesitation.

I proceed in on Sal alone on the penalty shot.

The Penalty Shot

The penalty shot is hockey's most suspenseful and dramatic play. The breakaway happens suddenly and without notice, a product of someone's mistake or a combination of mistakes, which in the heat of battle goes mostly unnoticed. But a penalty shot allows time for everyone's excitement to build.

The penalty shot is called by the referee when an attacker who is breaking in on the opposition goal without a defensive player between him and that goal is illegally prevented from getting a shot away or making a play on the goaltender. He may be tripped, grabbed, hooked, or interfered with in some other way.

A penalty shot can also be assessed when a player from the defensive team throws his stick in the direction of the offensive player breaking in on goal, or when a defensive player falls on the puck while in the goal crease, causing a stoppage of play.

When a penalty shot is awarded a team, play stops immediately. The puck is placed at centre ice and both teams go to their respective benches. The offended player is then allowed to skate in on the goaltender alone. His only restriction is that he must not carry or shoot the puck over the goal line before making a play on the net. If he does so, the try is ended.

Spectators rise to their feet as the anticipation mounts. With each stride the player takes toward the goaltender the suspense builds as one athlete's skill is pitted against another's. The arguments of armchair coaches about whether a shot or a deke would be best now end.

A deke to the left, a sharp move to the right, and the attacker sweeps the puck across the front of the crease just out of the goaltender's reach. The goaltender realizes he cannot reach the puck and holds his ground. Seeing that his move has not fooled the goalie, the shooter quickly sends the puck toward an exposed corner. A flick of the wrist—and the puck rests securely in the webbing of the goaltender's glove. The attacker is disappointed, but seventy-five per cent of these attempts fail. The edge is *always* with the goalie who refuses to commit himself first.

Changing On the Fly

Since play doesn't stop conveniently when players

Here I jump over the boards to replace a teammate while play continues.

are tired, the ability to change lines while play is on (on the fly) is an important art. Only change when (1) you have possession of the puck or (2) the puck is deep in the opposing team's zone. Changing must be done very quickly, so you must be alert to when it's your turn to go on the ice and who you will replace.

The Soviet teams use a clever play to change players on the fly. A Soviet player or group of players speed up ice, driving their opponents deep into their defensive zone. Then the Soviet puck carrier will turn and pass the puck to the Soviet defensive zone to a defenceman who deliberately stationed himself there when the rest of his teammates sped up the ice. As soon as this happens, the four tired players skate to the bench and four fresh players stream over the boards. They head back to their own zone to regroup, still in possession of the puck. With a couple of quick passes, they advance again, giving the fifth member of the group a chance to be replaced. In this manner, the team keeps possession of the puck while changing.

Playing Both Ways

A puck carrier, of course, thinks offensively, but he must also protect his team against the loss of the puck by thinking defensively. The player who is continually caught in the opposing team's end leaves his team at a disadvantage when he is too far down the ice to catch up to the play and backcheck.

Fans should note this particular aspect of the game and, as play moves from one end of the ice to the other, watch how players' responsibilities change to meet changing circumstances and changing possession of the puck. On a well-rounded hockey club, most, if not all, of the players on the team assume the dual responsibilities of offensive and defensive play, and carry both out well. It is the team that does not *think* or *play* both ways that cannot adjust to the constantly changing circumstances in a game.

Positional Play If each player plays his position properly, as shown in the wedge, and the effort is orchestrated by their coach or leader on the ice, the success of the team will be ensured. It is important to note that players must be flexible in the wedge but that any player who leaves his position should be covered by another player. Productive plays are not accidents, but the result of hard work and practice by forwards and defence-men who, acting together, form the plays as they

move up and down the ice.

When plays go well, it looks as though someone is quarterbacking the team. In football each player knows what offensive play is coming up, but in hockey each player must read his teammates' minds as the play moves down the ice and must adjust to the inability to actually communicate a play by calling it prior to its execution. This aspect of the game requires a great deal of sensitivity and concentration. For players to sense each other's moves ahead of time is almost like being able to tell the future. A player can only know exactly what each of his teammates is going to do in a given situation when he has played a long time with them and when they are accomplished hockey players who understand what play best suits any situation.

The Coach's Offensive Role

The coach plays an extremely important offensive role, for he must match the players on line with each other and also against the opposition. It is his keen eye and knowledge of the sport that judges players' abilities to complement each other. In a game, you will see that line match-ups are extremely important, as a coach will try to emphasize his team's strengths and also take advantage of the other team's weaknesses. Only the coach can provide this kind of leadership to his players, because he is the only one in a position to evaluate situations from outside the playing surface. As match-ups and line changes occur during the game, they are not noticed by the less sophisticated hockey viewer. Yet this seemingly effortless orchestration represents many hours of practice and many years of coaching that began when the coach first joined an organized team.

Coaching Children Our discussion of coaching would not be complete unless we looked at how a coach's role is different at different levels of a child's hockey growth. It's important to take a look at these roles to fully appreciate their importance to the player, for, as a player goes through growth stages, the coach must be able to meet the needs of each child's development.

For the very young player just starting out, it is important that the coach be a nice person who has the children's best interests at heart. He should provide them with a schedule and some leadership and guidance in getting their equipment on, being on time, and developing rudimentary skills. He must *not* put pressure on them, but simply make sure they have fun. At an early age, kids have enough problems just skating, handling the puck, and staying out of the way of the opposition. They should be out there just getting the feel of the puck, of skating, and of being part of a group. Many coaches put too much emphasis on too many technical things before the kids are ready to grasp even elementary skills.

Parents sometimes confuse kids, too! One is hollering "Pass!", another is hollering "Shoot!", while yet another is hollering "Check!", and the kids don't really know what they should be doing.

At all times the coach should be in control, teaching young players the proper attitude to take toward the game—outplay the opposition, out-skate them, out-think them, outposition them, out-check them, but do not try to intimidate them. The coach must be like a parent and a counsellor to the kids, and a disciplinarian to a certain degree. But mostly he must be their friend. When they are dedicated to a sport, kids will listen to a coach and believe him before they'll listen to and believe their parents. This trust must never be abused.

Of course as players graduate to higher levels and they gain the capacity to grasp the technical part of the game, they need someone who understands the game and knows when and why they are making mistakes, and who is able to communicate with them and point out their mistakes in a constructive way. That is the only way bad habits can be broken.

The importance of having people with the proper training and temperament to coach our kids at different levels cannot be overemphasized. The image projected by the coach to young and impressionable players must be positive in every way, for coaches teach about more than just hockey, they teach about life.

9

6
DEFENSIVE PLAY

Defensive play is vitally important to winning a hockey game. Yet it is rarely understood and even less often appreciated, especially by undereducated sports fans. It's much easier to identify with the player who puts the puck in the net than with the one who knocks the puck away with a poke check so that his team gains possession. The defensive player is often unheralded but is as necessary as the scorer to make a team complete, well-rounded, and capable of winning play.

In the last chapter you learned some of the ways to overpower the opposition offensively. This chapter will explain the ways to defend against such strong offensive drives.

The Defencemen   The defensive players serve as the last line of defence on the path to the goal-tender. Since they often skate backwards, they are in the best position to see the offensive play form as it comes out of the opposing zone and materializes in the neutral zone. So the defensive strategy rightfully centres around them, with all other players on the ice coordinating their efforts with the defencemen's.

The position of these players is extremely important, as you will see, for positioning is the key to neutralizing the offensive team's penetration into the defensive zone. It also provides the way to set up a break from this zone when the defending team regains possession.

Defensive Positioning

The ability of a team to force its opponent to make a play, especially one it doesn't want to make, provides the surest defence against attack. You can accomplish this by applying constant pressure to the attackers and sticking to your position. One of the best defensive positionings is to play a zone defence.

There are six areas (or zones) behind the blue line in the defensive zone that must be patrolled by the defenders to stop dangerous shots and passing plays by the attacking team.

The six areas are outlined as follows:

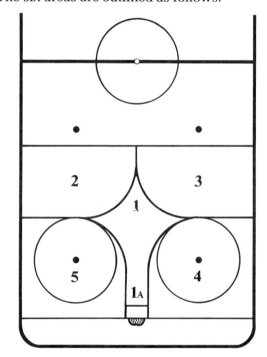

The next diagram illustrates the proper positioning for defending against an attacking team that has a player with possession of the puck in area 4.

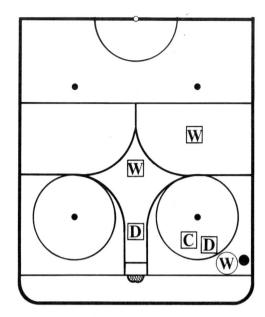

1. Two players chase the puck carrier. One takes the man, the other the puck (area 4).
2. A defenceman covers the front of the net (area 1A).
3. A winger covers the slot (area 1).
4. A winger covers the left point (area 3).

Notice that areas 2 and 5 are left uncovered. To get the puck to a teammate in area 2, the puck carrier would have to pass the puck through areas 4, 1A, and 1. This would involve a high risk that the puck would be intercepted. He would have to shoot behind the net to get the puck to area 5.

Obviously this defensive positioning has left the puck carrier with few passing choices, and the ones that he does have represent a minimal scoring threat.

With the zone defence, each player covers his area by adjusting either to the right or the left (effectively addressing the unbalanced wedge) according to the movement of the puck into an area. One defenceman *always* remains in front of the net when the other team has possession, and two players should be on the puck carrier at all times (one to take the man out and one to take the puck).

This defensive positioning closely resembles a zone or box formation because of the relationship of the defencemen to the forwards after the play enters the defensive zone.

Meet Them at the Blue Line One way of breaking up a play before it gets a chance to enter your zone is to meet the attackers at your blue line. There are two ways of doing this: (1) the non-staggered defence and (2) the staggered defence.

In the non-staggered defence, the defencemen line up straight across the blue line. In the staggered defence, one defenceman stands at the blue line, while his partner is slightly behind him in the zone. If the puck carrier gets around the defencemen in the non-staggered defence, he's in on the net alone, but in the staggered defence, the second defenceman is able to pick up this player as he moves around the first defenceman, since he is positioned deeper in the zone. The following diagrams illustrate this situation.

Non-staggered defence.

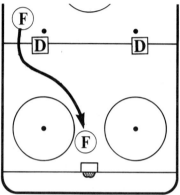

Staggered defence (with pickup).

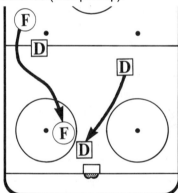

Keep the Man to the Outside It is the job of the defencemen to keep the puck carrier away from the middle of the ice. The further he is kept to the outside, the poorer the angle he will have for shooting on the net.

You can force the puck carrier to move to the outside if you can control his position on the ice. This is done in two ways: (1) cut off the inside by blocking the middle with your fellow defenceman, making it impossible for the puck carrier to split your defence, and (2) make sure your backchecking wingers position themselves so that the puck carrier is between them and the boards. In any case, only lateral movement and backward skating ability will allow you to use this strategy.

When you have kept the man to the outside, you are faced with two options as he skates deeper into your zone. You can (1) attempt to check him into the boards and then steal the puck, or (2) patiently wait for his move as you keep him close to the boards.

By following the first option you run the risk of missing him and taking yourself out of the play. But if you and a backchecking forward employ the strategy of keeping two men on the puck carrier, you will increase your chances of getting the puck. By following the second option, you stay closer to the play, but risk the puck carrier making a successful pass or positioning himself behind your net. This can be dangerous, because some puck carriers are quite adept behind the net, and your goaltender's vision is reduced when he must look behind the net to determine the puck's position, readjust his position when the puck is passed out, and then prepare for a shot. These adjustments obviously increase the chances of a score.

Therefore, it is important that you read the play correctly and react instinctively to the puck carrier's move when you keep the man to the outside. Your defensive partner must also assume his position in front of the net to back you up and be ready to intercept any passes from the puck carrier and clear the front of the net.

By working as a team you can successfully use the strategy of keeping the man to the outside to prevent any scoring attempts by your opponents.

Defensive play requires complete checking skills: (1) body checking, (2) stick checking, (3) backchecking, and (4) forechecking. All checking represents different methods of impeding or blocking the forward progress of your opponent toward your goal and then regaining possession of the puck.

We have seen that balance plays an important part in hockey. It is the aim of the defensive players to disturb this balance. What better way than to bump into an opponent with your body? It sounds rough and it is, and you must be able to take it as well as dish it out, as long as it is fair and clean.

Body Checking

The sudden, powerful, and deliberate collision of two well-conditioned athletes is one of the main attractions of hockey for fans. This violent body contact is not seen in so sustained a manner in most sports. This, coupled with the speed with which players thrust their bodies across the ice at

each other and their intention of crashing their opponent against the boards, heightens the degree of expectancy for both the fan and the player.

Open Ice Body Check One of the most attractive and difficult checks to perform is the open ice body check. It is difficult because the timing required to block the offensive player coming down the ice is critical. The check must be timed with such precision that you are able to make contact with the offensive player and take him out of the play, and at the same time dislodge the puck so that your team gets possession. Improper timing will not only allow the opposing team a chance to score, it can also make you look foolish in front of the fans and your teammates.

Roy attempts the open-ice body check and has me lined up.

His shoulder is thrown as I make my cut, and Roy just misses by the smallest of margins.

The margin was enough. Roy is completely out of the play and I am in on net alone.

Playing the Eyes and Chest. The surest way to increase your chances of body checking successfully is to first look at the oncoming skater's chest or eyes, using them as clues to where the body will go. During my playing days, players like Leo Boivin, Marcel Pronovost, and Pierre Pilote were masters at playing their men in this way, and many felt the hip checks of Dougie Jarrett when he read their moves through the eyes and chest.

Never, under any circumstances, look at the puck, or you will quickly find out that the puck carrier has gone around you.

As Roy skates in, I play his eyes and chest, keeping my body square at him.

There are many other types of open-ice checks that can be used to take the puck away from the attacking player. But before we pursue this further, you must understand that once the player carrying the puck is intercepted, it is your responsibility to control the puck and pass to a teammate or carry it into the opposing team's zone. Therefore, just as it is your job to disrupt your opponent's balance, it is also important that you keep your own.

Placement of the Body Some of the most effective checks are achieved when you are able to place your body between the puck and the puck carrier so that contact is made at the mid-point between these two. It is interesting to note the reason for this effectiveness. The stick, as we discussed before, is an extension of the player's body. By successfully cutting off this extension, you deprive the player of the ability to carry the puck effectively, and you have placed yourself in a position in front of the puck carrier so that you will be able to skate forward before the player who has received the body check is able to regain his composure and continue play. This manoeuvre is called "riding your man off the puck."

Preparation. Let's start by assuming that a player on the opposing team is carrying the puck toward you. To be able to make body contact with this player, you must be skating at the same or greater speed. Remember that this body contact should not be made with the hockey stick, nor by grabbing the puck carrier. You don't want to leave your team short-handed and *increase* your opponent's scoring chances instead of *decreasing* them.

The Hip Check One of the most dynamic body checks in hockey is the hip check. As the attacking player makes his move, watch his eye and chest movement as you skate backwards. Suddenly swing your hip quickly in the direction of the puck carrier and at the same time shift your entire weight as your skates point in the opposite direction of the check.

Timing is critical; your hip must catch the player at his mid-section and, as contact is made (crouched down and with your legs bent in the backward skating position), dig your blades into the ice to plant your feet, stop your backward movement, and give you strength and added balance as you bear the weight of the checked player. Since this check catches the skater off guard and he is hit below his centre of gravity, it will usually lift him off the ice and flip him over your hip.

Here Roy times the hip check perfectly as I attempt to go around him. He catches me at the midsection while moving sideways.

As the check is completed, my body goes over, breaking my forward movement.

The Shoulder Check   In the shoulder check, your shoulder hits the skater squarely, or with a glancing blow that causes him to lose momentum and balance. Shoulder checks are jarring for both players and must be timed properly to avoid a miss that would place you out of position.

To make a shoulder check, first stop your movement with a one-foot stop. Shift your weight to the forward foot, straighten your back leg, and turn your shoulder toward the puck carrier. When contact is made, shift your weight to the back leg to keep your balance.

Shoulder checks can also be used when you are skating forward toward an opponent. The speed of your forward movement will greatly increase the force of the check. Unfortunately, most players executing this variation lose their balance because they become too anxious and lunge forward at their opponent. Lunging will cause you to place your weight forward and lift your skates off the ice. Consequently, you will lose balance momentarily. This will take you out of the play, and the force of your check will be reduced.

Always remember to keep your skates firmly planted on the ice, meet your opponent's body with your forward momentum, and push your shoulder forward at the point of contact. This allows you to keep your balance and get the most from your check.

Board Checking   Not only can you check the puck carrier in open ice with your body or stick, but, like a boxer using the ropes, you can use the boards to your advantage.

If an oncoming offensive player cannot be stopped by open-ice body checking, or by stick checking, the only alternative left is to attempt to get him closer to the boards. Once you have done this, you can use the boards as an extra defence partner. Throw all your body weight against the

Here I board check Roy. Notice that he loses control of the puck. If a teammate followed me (two men on the puck) my teammate could easily gain possession.

puck carrier so that he is sandwiched between you and your "partner." Stay aware of the shooting curve and be sure that your opponent cannot reposition himself in this area.

Board checks, as can be imagined, create a resounding thud, much to the delight of fans. Sometimes the sound is more impressive than the check, but the fans thrill to these checks as the crashing noise and the wavering glass above the boards create an image of power unmatched in other sports. Doug Jarrett, while playing in Chicago for the Black Hawks, was one defenceman who could really make the ends of the rinks shudder. That's why he was nicknamed "Chairman of the Boards."

Riding Your Man into the Boards Although it is less dramatic than a full board check, an effective way of gaining possession of the puck is by physically directing the puck carrier into the boards and taking the puck as he hits the boards.

I then ride him into the boards and cut off his path. He loses possession . . .

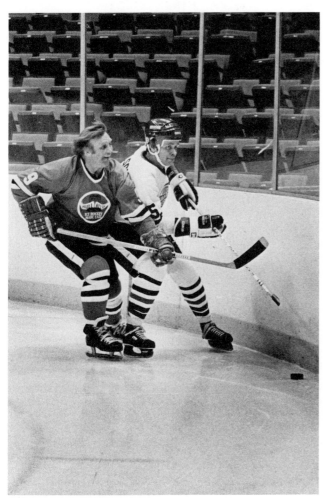

As Roy attempts to go around the boards, I place myself on his outside and get slightly ahead of him.

. . . while I continue to take him out of the play. (Remember, two men on the puck carrier: the first to take the man, the second to take the puck.)

131

Taking a Check Now that we have discussed checking the puck carrier, we must discuss what the puck carrier has to do when checked. Obviously you must attempt to avoid being checked, but not at the risk of shying away from the puck through fear. If you skate with your head up and don't take a pass while looking backwards, you can avoid a great many checks. But sooner or later you will be checked, and knowing how to prepare when an oncoming defensive player is going to check you is extremely important. You must be able to absorb checks so that you are not injured and so that you can give as much of a jolt to the checker as the checker gives to you.

It is therefore essential not to maintain a relaxed body posture when you are being checked into the boards. This will create a looseness in your entire body that can cause a severe injury. You should be able to receive the check and take the punishment by tensing all your muscles. Tensing the body makes two things happen: (1) your body becomes one solid block of hard muscle, and solid muscle reacts much differently than soft flesh (When running into some players during my career, I found it was like hitting a marshmallow, while others, like Gordie Howe, were like a brick wall!); and (2) your joints are protected and held together by elastic tendons and ligaments (preventing a separation).

It is also essential that the player checking the puck carrier against the boards not relax, so that he can come off the boards without losing momentum. If he does relax he can not only injure himself but will take himself out of the play and lose any opportunity to gain control of the puck.

When a player experiences these jolting and jarring body checks, he will appreciate all the equipment he wears. The protection afforded by this equipment is, as we previously noted, extremely important. It is also a comfort for a young player to know that he is adequately protected and that he need not favour an area where he may not have adequate protection and thus hamper his game.

Stick Checking

A less violent but equally important form of checking is stick checking. Stick checking is legal as long as it doesn't involve slashing, tripping, high sticking, spearing, cross checking, or other dangerous manoeuvres against your opponent.

The Sweep Check Hold your stick at the butt end with one hand and make a sweeping motion with

The sweep check: start the sweep with one knee bent, the other leg out to the side, and the stick blade flat on the ice pointing forward.

Sweep the stick across in front of your body...

...and the puck is dislodged from the attacker.

your stick to knock the puck from the puck carrier's stick. Since the hockey stick's length is 55 inches, this represents a large area that can be covered by the sweep of your stick in front of you and to your sides.

One drawback to the sweep check is that the path of the puck is unpredictable after the sweep, so that the chance of your gaining possession is low. To increase the sweep's radius and limit your loss of balance, bend your body at the waist slightly, and squarely face the oncoming skater. Your skates should be a comfortable width apart and your bottom arm positioned to meet the return sweep of the stick so that you will be ready to skate forward.

The Poke Check Hold the stick at the butt end with one hand. Stride forward and, with a poking lunge forward, attempt to dislodge the puck from the opposing player's stick blade with the blade of your stick.

The poke check: hold the stick straight ahead in one hand.

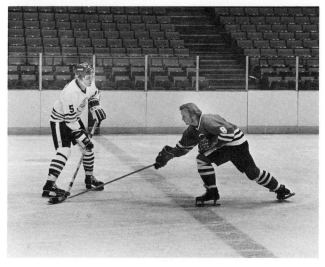

Lunge forward, knee bent, and remove the puck.

Both the sweep and the poke check must be timed accurately. Wait for the puck carrier to get close enough and then patiently wait for the proper moment to make the check quickly. Do not accidentally give the puck carrier advance warning that will give him time to move the puck from the area of the check and then take advantage of your now committed body position to move around and behind you.

The Stick Pickup You must first get close to the puck carrier. Then use your stick, which you must grip with both hands, to lift the puck carrier's stick so that he loses control of the puck. Either you or a teammate will then have a chance to take the puck from him.

The Hook Check The hook check is very similar to the sweep check. Hold your stick with both hands and hook your blade to the puck carrier's. At the same instant pull his stick away from the puck. Either you or a teammate will then have a chance to take possession. At the very least, the puck carrier will temporarily lose control of the puck.

The Stick as a Defensive Tool The art of stick checking shows that a hockey stick is not only an effective scoring tool, but also an effective defensive tool. Because of its length, it increases the area that a defensive player can cover without overextending or changing his skating position, which could cause a loss of balance and strength due to lack of leverage.

It is important to remember to exercise restraint when you use these stick-checking methods. Good offensive players can't wait for a player to commit himself so they can move the puck out of danger and quickly skate past a checker who is out of position.

A stick check, done with a little too much fervor, can become a high stick, a hook, or a trip, and thereby end the advantage it might bring to defensive play, if a penalty is called. When used properly, however, stick-checking techniques, combined with body-checking techniques, provide powerful ways to reduce the scoring threat of the opposing team.

A good offensive player can increase his value to his team by mastering these defensive techniques. The same is true of a defensive player who is able to carry the puck and shoot accurately, as well as performing his defensive job. This is the step that separates a fine team from a mediocre team. If a fan or young enthusiast playing the sport watches closely, he would see quite vividly that a sound and winning hockey team combines both elements. This gives a team the competitive edge that often makes the difference between winning and losing the game.

The Defensive Spirit

Defensive play can appear to be unrewarding. Very few defensive players receive the plaudits they deserve from the fans watching the game. There are two reasons for this: (1) the less astute fans fail to recognize the importance of defensive play, and (2) the more colourful skating and shooting aspects of the game receive greater attention from the fans and sportswriters. The importance of defensive play, however, should not be underestimated, nor should the players who specialize in this contribution to their team be looked at as of lesser value than their scoring counterparts. It is often said that a goal saved is a goal made.

Defensive players, because of the constant body contact that is necessary to their play, take and mete out a great deal of punishment. Obviously, a defenceman who is able to instill fear or respect in his opponent gains a psychological advantage over the opposing player. The opponent will be less apt to take liberties with him. Do not confuse this with a strategy of outright intimidation used to win games. It is usually these bully tactics that cause outbreaks of violence.

Retaliation All too often, when a player is checked, he retaliates. This retaliation can take many forms, but the most common is fighting. Hockey has developed a reputation for all-out brawls on the ice, and I can't help but think that this has hurt the sport. Then again, many of the fans who come to the arena would probably be disappointed if they did not see a fight during a game. This is unfortunate, because hockey holds many fascinating attractions for the fans—and fighting should not be one of them. When fighting does occur, it is unfortunate that it is sometimes in retaliation for a hard but legal check. Often a player will take liberties with the severity of his checking, and the player being checked will take exception to these liberties. The result is a confrontation.

It is the job of the referee to make sure that these confrontations are kept to a minimum and that he maintains control of the game so that such situations do not get out of hand. It is important for the young player to accept that he is going to check and be checked in return, and to view this as a fact and not as a personal affront to him. This attitude will prevent any unnecessary retaliation.

I am not advocating that players should not stick up for themselves, because in any sport some players will take liberties beyond what the rules allow. A player should develop respect in the league, so that these liberties do not become commonplace, and players who take these liberties should be discouraged from doing so by being penalized.

Backchecking

When your team is on the attack and loses possession of the puck, the forward skaters must backcheck, or skate back to cover their men. To backcheck effectively, you must place yourself between the man you are covering and the puck, and be close enough to intercept any passes and to eliminate your check from getting involved in the play. Obviously a player who does not backcheck leaves his team at a disadvantage. He is called a one-way player. A player who goes both ways is not a luxury, but a necessity.

As I skate up the boards, Roy backchecks, keeping me between him and the boards.

Forechecking

Once you lose possession in your opponent's zone but before you start backchecking, you must forecheck, or attempt to get the puck back from the puck carrier or make him make a bad pass so that one of your teammates can intercept the puck.

Use the stick-checking and body-checking techniques previously discussed to bottle up the puck carrier in his zone. But don't let all your forwards forecheck too deeply or they run the risk of getting caught deep in the zone. A quick pass out and your opponents will have a fast break and a three-on-two or two-on-one.

The success of your forechecking lies in following some basic rules: (1) don't all go in at once and get caught deep, (2) always keep moving and do not lose momentum and speed, (3) make yourself look as big as possible with your arms, legs, and stick stretched out as far to the sides and front as possible and, (4) know where your man is, so that if you must backcheck, you can pick him up immediately.

Covering Your Man

Covering your man may sound simple, but it is not. Remember, you're not shadowing the other player constantly, but playing your own game and reverting to this task only when forechecking or backchecking. Hockey is a team game—if someone is covering *your* man, you'd better be covering *his.*

Here I'm being kept wide by the placement of Roy's body, which cuts off my path to the goal.

As I look for the puck, Roy skates with me.

We've discussed your positioning while backchecking and forechecking. When the opposing team penetrates your defensive zone, you should closely check your man, and as he moves toward your net, you should stick to him like a magnet. After that particular play is over, revert to covering your zone. If you are a winger or a centre, be sure to help your defencemen. Keep aware of the position of the puck at all times so that you may quickly switch from defence to offence.

Other Defensive Moves

Clearing the Front of the Net One of the potentially most dangerous shots is the screen shot. To counteract this danger, defencemen must clear the opposition forwards or defencemen from in front of the goaltender so he is not screened and can see the shot coming from outer areas of the defensive zone. This is an extremely important and difficult task for the defencemen.

Clearing the Puck When there is a lot of offensive pressure it is sometimes wiser to relieve the pressure by shooting the puck down the ice to the opposing team's zone. This results in icing and a faceoff in your zone. Your opponents may regain possession of the puck but at least it gives you the time to regroup and organize your efforts.

Freezing the Puck Another alternative to clearing the puck is "freezing" it. The defensive player holds or freezes the puck against the boards with his skate or stick or body to obtain a stoppage of play and gain time to reorganize. Be careful not to freeze the puck unless an opposing player is fighting you for it, or you might get a penalty for delay of game.

Here Roy clears me from in front of the net.

As the puck is frozen against the boards with my skates, Roy attempts to pry it loose.

Penalty Killing

When your opponents have a power play, your job is to kill your team's penalty. You must maintain a strictly defensive attitude, since to attempt to play offensively when you are a player short will place you at a further disadvantage (unless, of course, you are a Gretzky or a Messier).

If you have possession of the puck, it is more important to use up time than it is to try to score a goal. Good stickhandlers will "rag" the puck—carry it up and down the ice—and so waste precious seconds. When a stickhandler senses that he will be checked and perhaps lose possession of the puck, he can pass it to a teammate or shoot it down the ice (a team with a penalty can "ice" the puck freely) so that the offensive team must first retrieve the puck, then re-group for another attack. All this takes time.

Let's assume that the opposing team has skated back and picked up the puck in their zone. Your penalty-killing forwards have followed them down the ice but have not gone so far into the zone that they would be caught in deep by a quick pass. These players must judge the other team's chances of getting the puck out and then must make an instant decision: Should they try to force a play by forechecking the puck carrier? Or should they turn back and start to backcheck?

The Criss-Cross If your forwards decide to backcheck, they should consider saving energy by criss-crossing in front of the net. To do this, both players make a wide sweeping turn and cross in front of the net, then backcheck on the wing opposite to the one they started from. This sweeping turn allows the forwards to keep their momentum and so gain an edge on their opponents as they move out of their zone.

The Blue-Line Fence As play moves into the neutral zone, the two penalty killers should be close enough to their men to counter any offensive move they might make or to intercept a pass. They must also make another important decision: Should they stay with their men and let the defencemen try to stop the puck carriers? Or should they form a blue-line fence?

If they choose to form a blue-line fence, they must skate ahead of their men, stop at the blue line, and turn to join with their defencemen in forming a four-man fence or wall that the attacking team must break through to enter your zone.

The following diagram illustrates the criss-cross and the blue-line fence.

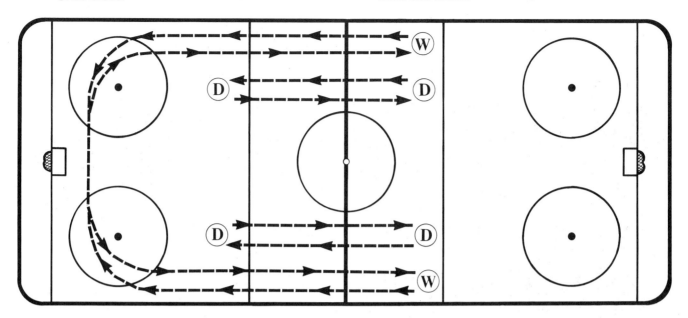

The Box

The Box If the attacking team has successfully entered your zone, the best tactic to use is the box. The two defencemen cover the area on either side of the goaltender while the two forwards cover the slot and point men. This positioning is in the shape of a box, although its sides continually change length as the puck moves around.

The defensive players must keep the attacking team on the outside of the box because the chances of scoring from there are weakest. The real danger zones are inside the box. Each player in the box must ruthlessly apply pressure, with the forwards forechecking at the point to force bad passes or hurried shots while the defencemen protect both the front and sides of the net.

The setup of the box looks like this:

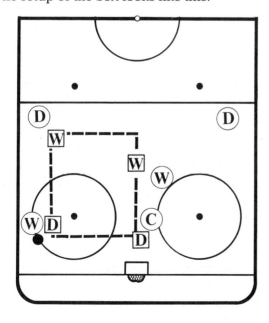

Blocks

We have seen the importance of positioning the body and stick in defence. Let's now add some refinement to the basic defensive skills, which, when used at the proper time, can complement the total defensive effort.

Body/Stick Blocks Using your body and stick to block shots and passes is an important tool that defensive players must master. There are many variations of this type of blocking.

One-knee block. Drop to one knee on the ice with your other leg bent forward in front of you. Face the shooter squarely, put your weight on the knee on the ice, and keep your arms and stick at your

The defenceman goes down on one knee, arms and stick at his sides, in front of the shooter.

sides, palms facing forward. Hold your stick to the side, with your hand at the butt end so that you can sweep or poke it at the puck carrier. Since you are down on one knee, it is easy to get up by straightening the bent knee in front and at the same time bringing up the other knee from the ice. Timing is important. You must know the exact moment to attempt this manoeuvre.

Two-knee block. Here, the same body position is maintained, but you drop down on two knees at the same time. It is harder to get up from both knees, but just dig one or both blades into the ice at an angle and straighten your knees. At the same time, spring to a standing position. Al Arbour, now the N.Y. Islanders coach, was a master at this.

Down on two knees with arms and stick at his side, the defenceman stops the shot.

Both these blocks require that you know exactly when the opposing player is about to shoot. If you drop too soon, an alert puck carrier can fake a shot and then move around you as you sprawl on the ice out of the play.

Body/Board Block   Position your body as close to the boards as possible to block the puck as it travels around the boards. The puck should then fall in front of you, and you will be ready to move up ice.

By placing his body close to the boards the defenceman blocks the elevated puck and places it in front of him.

Stick Blocks   Except for the flip pass, most passes are made along the ice. If you place the shaft of your stick on the surface of the ice between the passer and the receiver, you will be able to block the pass.

Your timing is critical. If you put your stick down too quickly, it will alert the passer and he will not attempt the pass. So you must be able to read the passer's body movement to detect the moment he will pass.

Body Slide   When all else fails, slide in front of the puck. If you miss, however, the slide will put you out of the play. If you commit yourself to sliding too quickly, your opponent will race by you. Although a properly timed slide can block

The defenceman slides both legs together in front of the shooter at close range (limiting the chance of injury from the shot).

shots and passes, it can also block your goaltender and deflect shots off your body at him.

When using the slide, both feet are lifted off the ice. The edges of the blades should be directed in such a way that the body hits the puck or stick of the oncoming player, allowing your forward motion to move you gradually down and in front of the puck's path.

Think Defence

The defensive techniques and strategies in this chapter should provide you with a sound base to add to your offensive skills. You should be able to think both offensively and defensively. I can't stress enough the importance of being a complete, well-rounded player. Such players are always wanted by any team. So don't just practise putting the puck *in* the net. Make sure you also practise keeping it *out*.

9

7 GOALTENDING

> *The goaltender has the hardest job in hockey. He is confined to an area of the ice that he must protect under all circumstances. He must be able to see and stop a small disc of vulcanized rubber travelling at speeds of up to one hundred miles an hour while opposing players and teammates mill about in front of him blocking his vision. He must play the entire sixty minutes of the game burdened with forty pounds of equipment, while maintaining total awareness of the flow of play. And he must be able to withstand the pressure of knowing that he alone is the last line of defence.*

You might well ask why anyone would want to tackle this position. The answer is that goaltenders are a different breed of player, and what attracts them to the position are the very things that deter others.

Most people assume that the kid who can't skate is shoved into the net. This is far from true, for the goaltender must be able to skate and, above all, maintain his balance. Some goaltenders have been known to be pretty good skaters, capable of giving the forwards a run for their money in practice sessions.

Goaltenders have always been a special kind of player. They all have their own way of handling the terrible pressure of their position so that they can meet the obstacles before them and come through in the clutch. I feel fortunate to have played in front of two of the very best. Glenn Hall became so intense before nearly every game that he caused himself to be sick to his stomach. The sicker he became the more sensationally he played! Tony Esposito took over from Glenn and in his first year with Chicago racked up an amazing fifteen shutouts! Tony became very quiet before a game; he wanted to talk to no one and wanted no one to talk to him.

The Goaltender and the Team

The Hot Goaltender A goaltender who is tough to beat or score on is called "hot" or "on." A hot goaltender can inspire a team with his play. Great goaltenders can keep their team in the game until their teammates finally come alive and start to play. Consistently outstanding play will build up frustration in the opposing shooters and eventually discourage them. At the same time, it will stir a surge of spirit that can be felt by all the goalie's teammates. A big save can wake up a team whose will to win has momentarily taken a seat on the bench.

But every goaltender has his weaknesses. If you are the shooter, watch the goaltender during the game to discover what these weaknesses are. You might note that he misses high hard shots on his stick side, for example. This should provide you with a clue for testing the goalie during your time on the ice.

If you are the goaltender, on the other hand, you must know your own weaknesses, so that you can compensate for them during the game, and work hard in practice to eliminate them.

Talking It Up A goaltender can increase his

worth when he "talks it up" with his players and encourages them. Say a defenceman lets a puck carrier in for a clear shot on net. After the save, if you "talk it up" positively with this defenceman, his embarrassment will quickly disappear and not affect his next play. This may sound trivial, but try to remember how *you* felt when you made a mistake in public and think how great it would have been to have heard encouraging words from the victim of your mistake.

Besides restoring the confidence of your defenceman, you can warn of oncoming attackers, of players moving behind your defencemen, of unchecked opponents, and of the many developments that can quickly occur in a game. So try to be vocal to encourage and direct your teammates.

The Stance

A goaltender assumes a distinct position when in the net. Your silhouette should resemble a Z.

- Your knees should be bent, with both legs kept together.
- Your backside should point out as in the backward skating position.
- Your upper body weight should be placed forward over your thighs.
- Your shoulders should face squarely forward, directly over your knees.
- Keep your head straight and forward.
- Keep your glove hand at your side, slightly out and ready.
- Hold the stick in the knockdown-glove hand with the blade flat on the ice in front of your joined skates.
- Distribute your weight evenly on each skate blade.

You must feel comfortable in this position, because you will hold it throughout most of the game. Your weight should be placed correctly in order not to cut off your breathing by limiting your lung capacity.

Your movements will be limited by the confines of your net and crease. The best movement, initially, is to move your skates alternately from the flat position forward slightly while standing erect and catching your balance. This will keep the blood in your legs circulating and your balance aligned.

In the Net

Stretching A goalie needs a wide range of motions in his legs, arms, and back to protect his net.

Front view of goaltender's stance.

Side view.

Rear view.

Thus, it is important that you perform stretching exercises before playing, and during your practice sessions and off-ice exercises. These exercises will keep you agile and supple, and will lessen the chance of pulled muscles and unnecessary soreness caused by strain. If you get a chance to see the Soviet Union play, keep an eye on Vladislav Tretiak. Watch the tremendous range of his movements while he warms up.

Housekeeping Goaltenders are careful to look after the ice surface in front of their net, and for good reason. Since you must get up and down quickly, you cannot have a surface that will trip you. Most goaltenders will scrape the ice in front of the net to make it rough and give them something to dig their skates into.

Playing the Angles Since pucks are never shot from just one position on the ice, you must adjust your position to that of the shooter to reduce the opening of the net he can shoot at. Look back to the shooter's curve in Chapter 4, which represented the best shooting positions on the net. No matter where the shooter is positioned on the curve, you must face the shooter squarely. By doing so, you will cut down, or cover, the greater portion of the net, thereby dictating the terms of the shot to the shooter. The move to face the shooter squarely is called "playing the angles."

Coming out. You can further limit the angle of the shot by moving out to meet the shooter. By advancing toward the shooting triangle you will reduce the amount of the net the shooter can aim at.

Commitment When the puck carrier gets in close to the net, do not commit yourself or make your move, for once you do you are vulnerable to a countermove by your opponent and, unfortunately, you will not have enough time to adjust. Don't be fooled by fancy dekes and other moves; the goaltender's game is a game of waiting and then adjusting to the situation—not the reverse.

The goaltender comes out to meet the shooter.

The Save

Stopping the puck from entering the net is called making the save. In a split second the goaltender must choose the proper save to block the puck, which may be travelling at over 100 miles per hour!

The poke save as the puck carrier moves in front of the net.

Saves fall into four basic categories: (1) the stick save, (2) the skate save, (3) the body save, and (4) the glove save.

The skate save.

The split save.

The goaltender sets up for the shot.

The puck is shot . . .

. . . and the save is made in the pads.

143

The glove save.

The butterfly save.

Rebounds Saves sometimes result in the puck rebounding back into play. Try to make the save so that you can clear the puck out of danger or fall on it, pass it to a teammate or to a spot away from the front of your net.

On occasion you will have to fall on or smother the puck to stop the play. Do this when you need to relieve the offensive pressure and have your team regroup.

After The Save When you make the first save, try to stay on your feet so that you are ready for a second and a third attempt. If you are sprawled on the ice, the puck can easily be lifted over you.

This advice does not apply to goalies who have reflexes like Glenn Hall's and Tony Esposito's. Both these goaltenders used the butterfly style of goaltending and relied on tremendously quick glove hands and reflexes. With the butterfly style you drop your legs down on the ice at right angles to your body with the front of the pads facing the shooter. This covers a great deal of the lower portion of the net. The large open area up high is looked after by those great reflexes and glove hands. You should note that this type of goaltender can be vulnerable to well-placed high shots.

The Goaltender as the Seventh Player

If you can skillfully control the puck around your net, you can be almost the equivalent of another player on the ice. However, you should know that if you stray from the protection of your crease, you are fair game and can be checked. Nevertheless, if you can gain possession of a puck that is shot in before an opposing forward can get it or can accurately pass it to a teammate, you will increase

your team's control of the puck, and, of course, the game.

There are two common situations where good stickhandling skills can help your team: (1) handling the shot into the boards and (2) handling the shot on net from the blue line.

These situations both indicate that your defencemen have cut off the play at the blue line and the puck carrier has been forced to make this play as a last resort. This should tell you two things: the offensive thrust has been broken, and the remaining players must react to this change of play. This should give you some time, something you normally do not have, so make the most of it.

The puck comes around the boards and the goaltender comes out with his stick blade toward the board.

If the shot is into the boards, you must decide whether you can play the puck. If you can, you must then decide how to handle the puck so that your team gains possession. Should you pass to a teammate? Should you stop and position the puck behind the net so that a teammate can set up the play? Should you shoot the puck out of the zone? In any event, you must make these decisions without hesitation. Remember, all of this is happening in a split second, you are wearing forty pounds of equipment, you are using a stick that is not designed for puck control, and you are leaving your net! So, you'd better be sure of your decision.

Once you have made your play, your next responsibility is to get back into the crease—and quickly! This is why a goaltender must be able to skate well and handle that big goal stick.

The Stick

A good goaltender can use his stick almost as well as the forwards and defencemen use theirs. You should be able to stick-check opposition players who skirt the borders of your domain. Don't be afraid to slide your stick at opposing players who try to manoeuvre from behind or from the sides of your net. You should also use it to poke-check players trying to move the puck in front of you.

Sensing the Net You must know where the net is at all times. If you stray, your path back will probably be made while you are skating backwards, without visual guidance.

This ability can only be mastered through constant awareness. Sometimes, you will see a goaltender hit the posts with his stick in order to measure where he is in relation to the net. When

Sensing the cage.

you go down and get back up, come out to reduce an angle, or cut down an angle in the crease, you must readjust your position constantly and be aware of where you are in relation to the net.

Protecting Your Crease You must ensure that uninvited visitors from the opposing team do not position themselves near your crease to screen you or deflect a shot. This is really the defenceman's job, but sometimes the goaltender must assist his defenceman or take it on himself.

The techniques used to protect the crease are shoving, pushing, and waving the heavy stick. Most of these measures are executed with a great deal of restraint and reluctance by goaltenders, although it does not always appear that way to the fans.

This is where goaltenders come in for a lot of criticism, since their vulnerability is obvious and their ability to protect themselves closely scrutinized.

Few goaltenders will take a direct swipe at a skater—but all will use some method to keep the skater honest and the front of the net clear. Right, Billy Smith?

Lifting the Puck Sometimes you can quickly clear the puck by lifting it out of the zone. This is especially useful when your team is killing a penalty, and is a skill that should be practised.

Pressure

Your ability to handle pressure will make the difference between playing well and losing your concentration.

To relieve pressure, some goaltenders go for a skate during stoppages of play, or do housekeeping. Some talk to the referee, and some even to themselves. But remember, concentration is essential to success in the nets, so reduce the pressure you feel any way you can.

Leadership

A goaltender is in the best position on the ice to see plays developing and alert his teammates to them. The ability to read these plays accurately comes from knowledge and experience as well as a natural facility that sets goaltenders apart. If a goaltender assumes the role of a leader on the ice that this ability creates, he will complement and assist the coach's efforts dramatically.

Remember that the goaltender is a unique player, subject to tremendous pressures. Often the outcome of a game—win or lose—rests on his shoulders alone. Underneath his layers of protective clothing and behind the unchanging expression of his mask, the goaltender in hockey holds perhaps the most dangerous and exciting position in any team sport in the world.

9

A MESSAGE TO PARENTS AND PLAYERS

As you have seen, ice hockey is a mentally and physically demanding sport that offers to its participants the challenge of performing well both individually and as a team.

When the young player skates onto the pond or rink for the first time, he is filled with the excitement of trying new skills. A bond between the player and the game is quickly formed, and the player's love for the game, his experience, and his determination to play well will often make other things secondary. Love of this sport, or any sport, must be put into the proper perspective, however, for all too often priorities can be misplaced, and a sport can become a substitute for family or education. The best possible way to experience the joys a sport has to offer is to be a well-rounded person.

A player's formative years, when his style, awareness of his body movement, and attitude toward himself and the game are developed, represent a critical period. Each individual enters a sport with certain natural abilities, and these abilities can be refined and nurtured. However, for parents to think that exerting pressure on a young player will create a superstar is both foolish and harmful to the child.

The following letter says it all.

Dear Mom and Dad:

I hope you won't get mad at me for writing this letter, but you always told me never to keep back anything that ought to be brought out in the open. So here goes.

Remember the other morning when my team was playing and both of you were sitting watching? Well, I hope you won't get mad at me, but you kind of embarrassed me.

Remember when I went after the puck in front of the net trying to score and fell? I could hear you yelling at the goalie for getting in my way and tripping me. But it wasn't his fault—that's what he is supposed to do.

Then do you remember yelling at me to get on the other side of the blue line? The coach told me to cover my man and I couldn't if I listened to you, and while I tried to decide they scored against us. Then you yelled at me for being in the wrong place.

But what really got me was what happened after the game. You shouldn't have jumped all over the coach for pulling me off the ice. He's a pretty good coach and a good guy, and he knew what he was doing. Besides, he's just a volunteer coming down at all hours of the day helping us kids just because he loves sports.

And then neither of you spoke to me the whole way home. I guess you were pretty sore at me for not getting a goal. I tried awfully hard, but I guess I'm just a crummy hockey player.

But I love the game. It's a lot of fun being with other kids and learning to compete. It's a good sport. But how can I learn if you don't show me a good example? And anyhow, I thought I was playing hockey for fun, to have a good time and to learn good sportsmanship. I didn't know you were going to get so upset because I couldn't become a star.

Love,

Your son.

The young player needs the support of his parents. Their encouragement and participation create an atmosphere in which he can succeed on the ice and at the same time develop his character and a sense of pride in his abilities and talents. It is unfortunate that this is often overlooked, and the full burden is placed on the coach, who is usually donating his time during these early years.

It is, of course, not an easy task to be a hockey parent. Arriving early at the rink for games and practices, driving many enthusiastic players in the car, and packing all the equipment can sometimes test parents' nerves. It all seems worth it, though, when you see your child perform on the ice—just as parental cheers add to the young player's joy in playing.

Parental criticism is a powerful tool, and should be used wisely and constructively. The ride home from a game should be a pleasant pick-me-up, not a negative review of your child's performance. Don't try to push him beyond his true capabilities.

Sit back and enjoy the sport and your child's ability to play. Honestly acknowledge his strengths and limitations. Be there to cheer in victory and console in defeat.

As for you players, keep in mind that your attitude is an important part of everything you do. Above all, you should enjoy playing the great sport of hockey. Remember, you've made a commitment to your team and yourself to do your best. That is all anyone can ask of you, or you of yourself.

9

ROY G. NELSON. A native of New York City, Roy Nelson played junior hockey in St. Mary's, Ontario, and semi-pro for a variety of U.S. teams. He was a candidate for the U.S. Olympic team in 1968.

After graduating from the City University of New York, he became a legal administrator and managing law clerk for several prominent New York firms and now heads his own company providing consulting services to the legal community in the law office management field.

He lives in East Meadow, N.Y., with his wife and four sons.

Photographer:

PAUL J. BERESWILL has been a sports photographer, specializing in hockey, for over ten years, during which time he has received more than 120 awards. His work has appeared in numerous magazines as well as several books.

Illustrator:

PATRICK FLAHERTY is a freelance artist who lives in Boston, Massachusetts.

Goaltender:

SAL MESSINA played on U.S. hockey teams in Russia and Czechoslovakia in the 1960s, played in the now-defunct Eastern Hockey League, and was the practice goaltender for the New York Rangers. He has worked with various cable networks in the New York area, and now provides colour commentary for Rangers radio broadcasts. He is also a sales executive for an aircraft supply firm.